THE BEST OF FROM OUR OWN CORRESPONDENT 1989/90

EDITED BY MIKE POPHAM

Broadside
BOOKS LIMITED
LONDON

Designed by Emma Axbey and Glen Coombes
            The Studio
            15 Soho Square
            London W1

Typeset by Winns
            Peterlee
            Co. Durham

Printed by Bath Press
            Bath
            UK

ACKNOWLEDGEMENTS

I should like to express my gratitude to the BBC's correspondents for their outstanding contributions to the programme this year; Catherine Bradley of Broadside Books, who commissioned this book; John Tusa for writing the Foreword; Bob Jobbins, Editor World Service News, for giving me the opportunity to produce the World Service edition of *From Our Own Correspondent*; Zareer Masani, Producer of Radio 4's *From Our Own Correspondent* who commissioned some of these pieces, and his colleague, Deborah Owen, Nancy Holloway, Ian Richardson, Tanya Motie, Nigel Hogan and Helen Thomas for their encouragement and support.

I am grateful also to the following for their invaluable help in collecting these pieces together for publication at such short notice; Janice Brand, Roubee Chettiar, Jackie Danczyk, Sharon Dews, Pippa Gwilliam, Jo Petty and Jackie Stainburn.

Finally, to my wife Catrina I owe a special debt. For several weeks she worked long hours into the night entering these pieces into her computer to meet the publisher's deadline. Without her, this book would not have seen the light of day.

PREFACE

One of the BBC's most successful radio programmes is Alastair Cooke's *Letter from America*. Hard on its heels must surely be *From Our Own Correspondent*. It is a programme of "Postcards from the World". Unlike real postcards, in FOOC the colour and the pictures are in the writing. The tone is personal, the information atmospheric, the result enlightening. Like real postcards, they come at unexpected times from unlikely places, telling improbable adventures. You can tell your friends by the postcards they write. Judging by these essays, BBC Radio listeners have many good friends.

John Tusa
Managing Director BBC World Service
London 10 September 1990

INTRODUCTION

Since March 1990 the Bush House News room has been responsible for producing *From Our Own Correspondent* on BBC World Service. The idea behind this book is to give readers an opportunity to sample a selection of the despatches filed for the programme, covering a momentous year in politics. We move from the aftermath of Tiananmen Square and the dismantling of communism in Europe, to the unification of Germany in October 1990. We also bring you some unexpected stories from those parts of the world which are all too often overlooked in the general media scramble to cover the main events of the year.

Mike Popham
Editor, *From Our Own Correspondent*
BBC World News
London October 1990

CONTENTS

Introduction

Acknowledgements

Preface

EASTERN EUROPE

Page

WESTERN EUROPE
Page

THE MIDDLE EAST

AFRICA

NORTH AMERICA

LATIN AMERICA

ASIA
Page

AUSTRALASIA

Contributors

EASTERN EUROPE

September	10	1989	Hungary opens border with Austria
October	3	1989	East Germany closes border with Czechoslovakia after 13,000 citizens flee to the West
October	18	1989	Erich Honecker resigns as head of East German Communist Party: replaced by Egon Krenz
November	9	1989	Berlin Wall falls
November	10	1989	Tudor Zhikov ousted as Head of Bulgarian Communist Party
November	24	1989	Czech leadership resigns after mass demonstrations in Prague
December	6	1989	Egon Krenz resigns
December	17	1989	Demonstration in Timisoara, Romania, crushed; thousands killed
December	25	1989	Nicolae Ceausescu, Head of Romanian Communist Party, and his wife Elena condemmed to death and executed
December	3	1989	President Bush of USA and President Gorbachev of USSR declare Cold War over
December	29	1989	Dissident Playwright Vaclav Havel sworn in as President of Czechoslovakia
February	7	1990	Communist Party of USSR relinquishes Monopoly of power after modification of the constitution
February	12	1990	Ion Iliescu confirmed as Romanian President
March	14	1990	Gorbachev elected First Executive President of the USSR
May	29	1990	Boris Yeltsin elected President of Russian Federation
July	1	1990	Abolition of fortified border between East and West Germany, merger of the two economies

July	6 1990	Resignation of Bulgarian President Petar Mladenov
August	3 1990	Arpad Goencz elected President of Hungary
October	15 1990	Mikhail Gorbachev wins Nobel Peace Prize

On 18th October, it was announced that the seventy-seven year old Erich Honecker was stepping down to make way for Egon Krenz. On his first day in office he announced changes in East Germany's severe travel restrictions, but Egon Krenz still had a long way to go before commanding the affection of the East German people.

EGON KRENZ - THE TEACHER'S PET

BEN BRADSHAW   BERLIN   21 OCTOBER 1989

I f there were opinion polls in East Germany, I could say with more confidence that Egon Krenz would have been most people's last choice as leader. There are a number of reasons for his unpopularity. No-one likes a teacher's pet. Egon Krenz made a career of ingratiating himself with the country's former leader, Erich Honecker. Mr Honecker for his part made no secret of his admiration for his protege, nor of his desire to see him in the driving seat once he left. Then there is Mr Krenz's age: at 52 he is a spring chicken in East German terms, where the average age of the Politburo is 68... so he is regarded as a bit of an upstart too.

A much more serious impediment for Mr Krenz is his political record. It is not just that he was known as a hard-liner, but that he seems to have gone to extraordinry lengths in the past to confirm it. After the Tiananmen Square massacre, when China was reaping the wrath of the world, communist countries included, Mr Krenz headed a delegation to Peking where he warmly congratulated the leadership there on the splendid way in which they had put down the counter-revolution.

For the last few years, Egon Krenz has been the man in charge of maintaining the ideological fibre of East Germany's youth. Never before have

16

so many young people wanted to leave the country. There was a story last year that Mr Krenz intervened personally to get two boys at an East German school removed and punished because they had questioned the wisdom of government policy. They had asked in a class whether it was appropriate to celebrate a day of peace with an exhibition of military hardware and goose-stepping along Unter den Linden. Mr Krenz apparently heard this blasphemy from his sons, who attended the same school. It seems teacher's pets run in the family.

But by far the biggest obstacle in the way of Mr Krenz finding a place in the hearts of the people is his association with East Germany's all-powerful internal security system, and especially with its hated plain clothes police, or Stasi - an abbreviation of the word for state security service - Staatsicherheitsdienst.

There is a joke in East Germany that if the Stasi were disbanded, half the population would be out of work. Some experienced commentators estimate that 30% of the population either work for the Stasi or are part-time informers. True or not, the numbers don't really matter. As long as the East Germans think it, the desired effect is achieved.

I have been in a restaurant with a group of about ten East German friends, each of whom during the course of the evening has been identified behind their backs by one of the others on the table as a Stasi. Wives have even accused husbands, and vice versa. The effect of this paranoia is, as you can imagine, devastating to the mutual trust needed to sustain a close relationship. I stayed with a young woman in Leipzig recently, who had been recommended to me by friends in East Berlin. I have since learned she was a Stasi spy. I don't really mind, as I didn't compromise myself in any way and she was quite happy to introduce me to all the right people - supporters as well as critics of the system.

Most Stasis though, are easily identifiable. They are the men in their late teens, twenties or thirties who idle about in small groups at the scene of any demonstration or potential trouble, trying to look as if they are doing nothing more than passing the time of day ... white socks, slip-on shoes, rather nasty slacks, and nylon bomber jackets. When Mr Gorbachev came, they put on leather ties.

I was recently standing on East Berlin's Alexanderplatz, where I had been told there was to be a demonstration. I milled around in the unusually dense crowd of people waiting for something to happen. Then, all of a sudden, several of those people started shouting and unfolding banners. No sooner had they done so, than elements of the crowd that one might easily have taken for potential demonstrators pounced violently, dragging the protesters off to waiting police buses. Some of those fleeing to West Germany in recent months have, no doubt, been dispatched by the Stasi. Some will act as plant, others as propaganda material when they return home in a blaze of publicity to tell of the horrors of life in the capitalist west.

There are signs that Mr Krenz is aware of the harm these state thugs do to his image. Their presence at recent demonstrations has been much scaled down. Soon, the Stasi will be a thing of the past - rather like the Nazis after the war. More recently, the Stasi equivalants in Poland and Hungary have simply disappeared into obscurity, protected by their friends and families for whom they have long provided protection as a kind of anti-persecution insurance policy. If they do go, the word 'Stasi', more than any other, rather like the word Gestapo, will remain as a reminder of the system most would prefer to forget.

When Hungary pulled down the last vestiges of its barbed wire border that had separated it from the West, a chain reaction was accelerated that ignited pro-Democracy movements across Eastern Europe. However quietly the Hungarian revolution unfolded, the anguish caused by the economic and political restructuring of the country was nevertheless acute.

HUNGARY: THE FALLING OF THE RED STAR

SALLIE ECROYD   BUDAPEST   2 NOVEMBER 1989

Hungarians, if one can generalise, are many things. Quick witted, cultivated, full of black humour with flashes of genius, passion and inventiveness that have produced Liszt rhapsodies, Bartok concertos, a nation of poets, chess players and the Rubik Cube.

What they are not noted for is their joie de vivre. A pre-disposition to brooding melancholy and deep-seated pessimism are often offered as the cause of the suicide rate - since the last century one of the highest in Europe - and so accepted that there is barely any stigma attached to trying to kill yourself. The National Anthem, a beautiful, haunting melody which often reduces its singers to tears, swells with pathos: "Please God, we have already atoned for our past." Atoned the Hungarians could be said to have done. A deep sense of history means that every school pupil knows and lives a string of defeats. Invasion by the Mongols; occupation by the Turks; and most recently and tragically, the crushing of the 1956 uprising against Stalinist cruelty.

Right now, however, the people do have cause to be despondent. Their leaders have been spelling out warnings of doom and gloom over the economy. The danger of total collapse, the need for big redundancies and further sacrifice from the workforce; the inevitability of a continuing and sharpening decline in living standards. Almost all Hungarians already do two or three jobs to make ends meet. The air traffic controller, when he has finished directing aeroplanes into landing, copes with the traffic of the city as he turns himself into a taxi driver. The hairdresser takes in a neighbour's sewing; the bank teller starts an evening's work of translation... and that is before the next round of across-the-board price rises due in January.

But if Hungarians are not breaking holes in walls - and they did that months ago anyway with the tearing down of the Iron Curtain on their border - there is still a tangible sense of dismantling - the dismantling of a communist system and the party state. When delegates to the ruling party's congress transformed themselves into the Socialist party, they said they would leave the country until next year's free elections. No sooner had they uttered the words than they promptly disappeared almost entirely from public view.

T he party leader for only sixteen months, Karoly Grosz, solemnly returned his BMW to the party headquarters on the River Danube, packed his belongings and left for good. The ugly grey concrete building known to Hungarians as The White House has lost its imposing aura as the seat of all power. The ordinary person who used to be diverted well away from it by uniformed guards can now stroll right up to the front door. The lights don't burn late at windows these days; the building seems deserted and forlorn. The red star is meanwhile being painstakingly lowered from its heights on public buildings throughout the country. Even the state news agency began a recent report with the words: "Contrary to rumour, the Hungarian Socialist Party has not collapsed."

At that time, only 15,000 of the Communists' former members had signed up with the new party. The figure has since risen to over 30,000, but it still means that almost 700,000 have decided not to bother. Some of those were undoubtedly among the crowds belting out the Internationale, and punching closed fists into the air when Mr Grosz told a packed hall he would help regroup the old Communists into a party of their own, but most appear to be sitting back in relief. No more compulsion after forty years to belong to a party, or to play a role in politics.

Many who were faithful to the old party and its goal of full employment, now face redundancy themselves. As one high-ranking journalist on a state newspaper said: "I can't plan a year ahead any more. I know that after the state elections I'll be swept out of the Communist party even though I rose for most of my career as a non-party member."

There are hundreds and thousands more like him, but as they prepare to vacate their offices, some figures among the opposition are already preparing to move in. Gathering in parliament these days they can be seen strolling around the corridors, or standing in the shafts of light under the building's magnificent gilded dome. Among them is Mr Jozsef Antall, leader of the opposition Democratic Forum, already looking for all the world like a Prime Minister.

Radical political changes and mass pro-democracy demonstrations in November 1989 threatened one of the most orthodox Communist states in Europe for the first time in four decades.

BULGARIA'S ROAD TO REFORM

NICOLA CARSLAW   SOFIA   23 NOVEMBER 1989

Tozhkovism is the new buzz-word in Bulgaria. It is spat out with gusto. It derives from the name of Todor Zhivkov, who was deposed in a spectacular palace coup earlier this month. At last Saturday's mass demonstration - the biggest of its kind in Sofia for four decades - the 100,000 or so pro-reform protesters chanted with venom: "Down with Stalinism! Down with Hitlerism! Never again Tozhkovism!"

One of the speakers, the dissident poet Blagadi Mitrova won rousing applause and bitter laughter when she declared: "Zhivkov - he turned our land of roses into a land of sclerosis."

Now that he is gone, the people are baying for his blood. They have heard how he lavished money on private comforts and holiday homes. Whereas the former King Boris had four residences, Zhivkov had thirty. His despised playboy son, Vladimir, is said to have gambled away millions of dollars in casinos in the West. Zhivkov's favoured party cohorts, many of whom still wield influence at regional level around the country, have amassed great wealth and privileges.

Time and again I was told by Bulgarians that Zhivkov left a legacy of corruption, and should be put on trial. But it seems unlikely that trials will be held immediately. For one thing, there are too many members of the old guard still in power, and they might not escape implication in a damaging corruption scandal. And for the other, no-one is saying where Zhivkov is. Rumours are rife. Some say that the 78-year old hardliner is dead from a heart attack; others that he is under house arrest; others that he has fled the country and done a Marcos - a reference to the late leader of the Philippines.

The most likely story is that he is in retreat in one of his many palaces. I tried to visit one on the outskirts of Sofia, but couldn't get near. The vast concrete monstrosity is perched on the top of a hill, shrouded in conifers, surrounded by fences and guarded by stony-faced soldiers. I wasn't the only one trying to approach - curious diplomats were also there. A casually dressed man drew up in a Volga with diplomatic numberplates, and asked me in a Russian accent if this was the home of Todor Zhivkov. "Yes" I said, and he asked "Is he there?" "That's what everyone wants to know," I replied. The man strode off into the parkland, just as another two diplomatic cars arrived. No doubt the occupants' respective foreign ministries are anxious for information...

They are perhaps not as anxious as the many regional Communist Party executives dotted around the Bulgarian countryside. Appointed by Zhivkov, they would present the only real opposition to the new leader, Petur Mladenov. They must be feeling particularly uncertain, for if Mr Mladenov is to survive and retain the popular support he has broadly gained, he will have to change considerably these official power bases.

If he succeeds at that, he is still not out of the woods, by any means. Thirty five years of Tozhkovism have left Bulgaria with a huge budget deficit, a massive currency debt and a completely disillusioned people.

*For over forty years, the German Secret Police, or Stasi, had maintained a
grip of terror over the citizens of East Germany. It was the most detested
manifestation of the old Communist regime. In the early heady weeks of
the crumbling of East German communism, haphazardly-formed
Citizen's Committees representing People's Power began to turn the tables.*

SETTLING SCORES WITH THE STASI

TONY PATERSON   DRESDEN   16 DECEMBER 1989

The most hated structure in the once beautiful city of Dresden is still
the offices of the city's state security police - the dreaded Stasi. It is a
hideous concrete and glass box of a building bristling with aerials, steel
doors and surveillance cameras, set between grey crumbling villas on the
banks of the River Elbe.

It was from here that until only a few days ago, the Stasi - a state unto its
own in East Germany - kept the people of Dresden at heel. Arrest, torture
and constant surveillance by a huge net of informers ensured that the Stasi
maintained control of the whole population. Even the country's present
Prime Minister, the Dresden Communist Party chief Hans Modrow, was said
to be on the Stasi files, but now at the Dresden Stasi headquarters all that has
changed.

The outer walls of the compound are now covered in a riot of gaudy
graffiti: "cowardly dogs"; "no more political prisoners"; "pigs" and,
sarcastically, "retirement home." A huge red, green and gold flag of the East
German opposition movement has replaced the single red flag that used to
fly over the building. When we asked to be shown inside at the main
entrance, the green-uniformed People's Policeman in a bearskin cap
immediately deferred to another man in a blue anorak and a beret, who wore

an armband bearing the name of the new Forum Democracy Movement.

Ten days ago, an angry crowd of Dresdeners beseiged the Stasi headquarters and demanded the right to be given their Stasi records. They burst into the building, began ransacking the offices and threatened Stasi officials and their families. Since then, the Stasi headquarters has been under the joint control of so-called citizens Committees, comprising opposition members and a handful of ordinary policemen.

From one of the former interrogation rooms on the ground floor, a waiter in stonewashed jeans called Michael Witowski maintained uneasy control over the premises, issuing orders to frightened-looking thuggish police officers. He told us how lorryloads of guns and hand grenades were being removed from the building to secret locations throughout the city. The thousands of Stasi files were now sealed off on upper floors, awaiting careful examination by a joint commision of government and citizen's Committee members. At the same time, he said that ten top-ranking Stasi officers were under house arrest, whereas the remainder had stayed at home, evidently too frightened of people's retribution to dare to return.

The same form of People's Power is being enforced at Stasi headquarters throughout East Germany, and as a result the government has pledged to disband the twenty-two thousand Stasi members... but not before time. Dozens of leading Stasi men have been beaten up by vengeful protesters, and one top official shot himself dead when a lynch mob invaded his headquarters.

East Germans, it seems, are more determined to settle scores with their secret police than any of their counterparts in Hungary, Czechoslovakia and Poland. From inside the Dresden Stasi headquarters, Mr Witowski offered this explanation: "The Germans are by nature very thorough, but the Stasi carried this to an extreme - we just want to get our own back."

Just how thorough the Stasi was until a short while ago could be learned from the thousands of letters now pouring into the Dresden Citizens' Committee. They provide an avalanche of miserable evidence of the treatment meted out by Stasi men to ordinary people. One man's testimony told how he was arrested by a Stasi snatch squad simply for photographing a line of policemen at one of the recent pro-reform demonstrations. He was taken to Stasi headquarters, stripped naked and made to run a gauntlet of truncheon-wielding officers. Then he was taken to a nearby prison and made to stand for twelve hours spreadeagled against a wall. After that, he was held incommunicado for a further two days without food in a room with 600 other prisoners and only one filthy lavatory. Finally, he was released without even being told why he had been arrested in the first place. Others were evidently not so lucky: one of the slogans now on the walls of the Dresden headquarters asks the question: "Where are the files on Paul Suchow and Rolf Schneider who were tortured to death here?"

In Dresden the Stasi are said to have kept a file on every single member of the population. Just how they managed to do this was made clear to me just before I left the Dresden headquarters. I was handed one of the thousands of little leaflets found in the building. It was a standard letter given to all obedient Stasi informers and it read: "In recognition of your exemplary contribution to the maintenance of state security in the German Democratic Republic, your account has been credited with the sum of five thousand marks" (the equivalant of three months' average wages).

It was signed by the Dresden Stasi Chief Major - General Boehm... but of course he is now under house arrest.

After the sudden exhilaration of the Christmas revolution in Romania, Romanians and their interim leaders learnt the difficulties of establishing democracy in a country without a democratic tradition. Meanwhile, the Romanian people cautiously began to explore their new freedom, unsure as to how pervasive the influence of the Securitate, might still be.

THE FIRST STEPS OF FREEDOM

GRAHAM LEACH　　BUCHAREST　　18 JANUARY 1990

Bucharest is the only airport I have ever travelled through where you slide your suitcases through an X-ray machine on arrival as well as on departure. That reflects the degree of nervousness here about lingering elements of the Ceausescu regime mounting a counter-attack, possibly assisted by mercenaries from abroad.

The leading members of the National Salvation Front are closely guarded. They are convinced that Securitate members are still at large; trained snipers switching from apartment to apartment, biding their time. Indeed on Tuesday afternoon, while I was interviewing a young fighter in the revolution outside the Central Committee building which he and others had stormed, one of his comrades appeared to tell us that they had just captured another Securitate man who for three weeks had hidden in Ceausescu's network of underground tunnels.

Nervousness and anxiety among the Front's leaders perhaps explain last weekend's disarray, when the Communist Party was outlawed on one day; the decree annulled on the next in the face of a small, though noisy demonstration outside the Front headquarters. Two lessons were learned that night: the Salvation Front vowed never again to bow to the mob, while the people of Romania came to appreciate the fragility of their democracy. The most stunning impression I have gained here these past ten days is just how patient the Romanians are with their new interin leaders. Their actions may strike some people in the West as somewhat amateurish, but not Romanians, breathing the air of freedom for the first time. As one student said to me: "You have to understand just how horrible our lives were under Ceausescu."

A Romanian couple invited me to dinner, where their apartment and their conversation betrayed something of how the dictatorship had affected them. They pointed to a corner of the room hidden behind a curtain. The wall was stained black from the fumes which had belched out of a paraffin heater they had acquired to heat one room during the cold winters when Ceausescu ordered the radiators to be cut off. The heating is now back on, while the couple can burn more than one light bulb.

I was shown a photograph album of pictures taken by the husband on a trip to England. His wife, who had never travelled abroad, was forced to stay at home during his absence. The pictures were not like those of most tourists to Britain - photographs of Buckingham Palace, The Houses of Parliament, and so on - no, these were almost entirely pictures of well-stocked shop windows in British towns and villages - the butchers, the greengrocers and the newspaper stands.

That answered my next question to him, which was how, during the years of tyranny, the Romanians knew that there was a better life out there somewhere, given that their television screens were each night dominated by sycophantic tributes to Ceausescu. At least the East Germans could view the prosperity of the West on West German television. "It was by word of mouth," he said, "those of us allowed abroad came back and spread information."

Video tapes did reach the country despite the censorship, as did video recorders. In fact, anyone sent a VCR from abroad would hope to receive two - one for himself, and one to sell on the black market to pay for the first one. A leading Romanian sportsman told me that whenever he went abroad he would return with suitcases packed with goods unobtainable in his own country - denims, Beatles records, etc, which when sold would pay for his entire trip.

As I leave Romania after this, my first visit, I am struck by the sad thought that the couple who invited me to dinner, both in their sixties, will only have the winter of their years to enjoy the freedom denied them by Ceausescu. At least the young people have their lives in which to hope for and begin to build a new, democratic Romania.

Two months after the revolution in Romania, the country was still in ferment. Fear of the old guard provoked a conflict between the army and the government, which the army won. There is now a new, strong role for the army in dictating the course of Romanian politics.

THE GUN AT THE HEAD OF ROMANIA'S REVOLUTION

ALEX BRODIE   BUCHAREST   28 FEBRUARY 1990

The soldiers shuffling into place to make their protest outside government headquarters were a poor, bedraggled crowd. They were conscripts from Topraiser on the Black Sea. They had been working on the construction of a new port at Constanca; they had, in fact, been virtual slave labour. That was how the late dictator, Nicolae Ceausescu, had used the army - conscripts were a cowed and compliant workforce, and they didn't cost anything, apart from food and accommodation. As the appearance of these men attested, that needn't cost much.

The men from Topraiser felt that they had been forgotten by the revolution, and they had come to the capital to demand some basic, civilized standards. "We have no water to wash in or drink" said one, "we have a bath once a month. We have no heating. We sleep in the clothes we stand up in. We've all got lice."

The soldiers weren't alone. During a turbulent two weeks, Victory Square saw many protests, petitioners coming to court to have their grievances heard. it had medieval as well as revolutionary overtones. On one occasion there was a sad little column of blind people tapping their way around the Square, asking for decent treatment and jobs.

But one protest was of a different order altogether, and it rocked the government - for it was by the strong, not the weak. It was made by a group of army and air force officers from Timisoara, the place where the revolution began, and they were articulating demands which echoed fears deeply felt in the population at large. It soon became clear that these officers were in fact speaking for all but the very highest in the armed forces, and in three days they established that the army was a force to be reckoned with. The government, led by President Iliescu, had metaphorically a gun to its head. It gave in; it had no choice. It could now be argued that the armed forces have shaken off the humiliating political control of the communist era and established a position of respect; certainly the expectations that ordinary civilians now have of the army are great.

It was Ceausescu himself who had the job in the 1950's of reorganising the Romanian army into a communist force. He purged it, killed officers, and built the Commissar system. The all-pervasive security system became the power in the land, and not the army. Members of the Securitate were paid considerably more than their equivalent ranks in the armed forces. They were a Praetorian Guard, feared and resented by the army. The army sided with the people to win the revolution, but the revolutionary government then appointed several old guard military men to lead the army.

The one who caused most resentment, and eventually prompted virtual mutiny was Defence Minister General Nicolae Militaru. Now he had fallen out with Ceausescu some ten years before, but according to a book by Ceausescu's then Intelligence Chief, Ion Paceka, who defected to the United States, that was because Militaru was caught being recruited by Soviet Intelligence.

Militaru became a symbol of all the other appointees who had dodgy links with the past, or who had played a dubious role in the days of the revolution. Younger officers revolted, and won a new Defence Minister and promises of a purge. However, two subsequent incidents highlight the continuing worries about totalitarian methods. Last Sunday a small group of young people, some with an unsavoury rent-a-mob aspect, broke free from a peaceful protest and invaded government headquarters, where they gratuitously smashed windows and ransacked offices. The next day, in sinister response, several thousand miners came charging up to the capital to back the government and shout that there was no need to tolerate political parties, in a torchlight night-time rally addressed by the president. Those overtones were distinctly demagogic.

Many civilians, heartened by the army's successful confrontation with the government, now look to it to guard against any new glimmerings of dictatorship. "The people must never doubt that the army is with them" declared the new Minister of Defence. What is clear now, which wasn't two weeks ago, is that whatever course Romania takes will have to be taken with the consent of the armed forces. General Victor Stanculescu - a Minister of Defence in effect chosen by the army - is suddenly one of the most powerful men in the land.

At the end of February the British Foreign Secretary Douglas Hurd visited Hungary - and praised the Hungarians' pioneering role in the revolutions of the past months that have brought communism crashing down in Eastern Europe. Less noticed in the outside world, the Hungarians have also been doing pioneering work in a very different field - in teaching crippled children and also adults to walk.

HUNGARY TEACHES THE CRIPPLED TO WALK

MARK BRAYNE   BUDAPEST   1 MARCH 1990

D anielle Bowen-Slark is an intelligent, bright-eyed 12-year old from Orpington near London, with just one problem - she has cerebral palsy. Until two months ago, Danielle had spent her life immobilised on the floor, in bed, in a wheelchair. Until, that is, her parents finally gained her a place at the Peto Institute of Conductive Education in Budapest.

They had waited for two years; now, with money raised by patrons at, of all places, their local pub in England, the Rose and Crown. Now they are paying 24 dollars a day for five hours of intensive instruction for Danielle. Where doctors in Britain had said she would be paralysed for life from the neck down, Danielle is now already standing. Within weeks she will walk.

Danielle was one of several dozen children, both foreign and Hungarian, introduced at the Peto Institute to Judy Hurd, wife of the British Foreign Secretary. Douglas Hurd's office is now mobilising five million pounds of government money and five million more of private funding to help Hungary build a much larger institute to be ready in three years' time. At any one time the Institute is already teaching some 100 children from Britain among the nearly two thousand victims of cerebral palsy, multiple sclerosis and even Parkinson's disease who come here for treatment.

The story the Institute's director, Dr Maria Hari, has to tell is an extraordinary but also controversial one of perseverance and of love. British physiotherapists are still slightly dismissive about Dr Hari's claims to special success - but for nearly forty years, the Budapest institute has been enabling children who had been written off by conventional doctors to walk.

How is it done? Danielle when we met her was the oldest in her class. The youngest two in the group were six, identical twins from Australia, also with palsy. Helped by their mothers behind them - for it is the parents at least as much as the children who have to learn - all were on their feet, gripping the rungs of special high-backed chairs. Their Hungarian conductor, as the teachers are called, was leading them in song - the words "We're standing up tall" - and getting the children to raise first their right arm, then their left, then to look to the left and look to the right. It may sound simple, but there was triumph written on their faces as they realised what they could do.

Another British girl, 10-year old Mary Nugent, had been at the Peto Institute for three months. She had arrived with her right arm locked behind her back, and had never been able to get out of her wheelchair. Now, admittedly with some difficulty, she was walking backwards and forwards between two parallel bars. Her mother was almost in tears as she told us of their shared joy at Mary's new mobility. Mary and Danielle are old by Peto standards. Dr Hari says potentially crippled children should really come before they reach school age.

We were shown a nursery class, where seven mothers following the instructions of their Hungarian conductor were taking their little ones through a series of detailed exercises more like intensive play, teaching them to react to song, to the sound of a tin whistle, to ordinary talk. The idea is never to let the children even develop the feeling that they are handicapped at all. The intensity of the attention they're given is remarkable - five hours at a time non-stop for both parent and child. In the next kindergarten class three and four-year old children with canvas bags around their necks were playing at picking up pieces of paper coloured like leaves, but also then at cutting real mushrooms. The next step is a real school class, where children, some with greater difficulty, some with less, were learning to write.

It was a moving experience to see the determination of the children and the love as much of the conductors as of the parents. Dr Hari's aim is to enable the children to leave the Institute and continue normal lives at home and a normal school education - and in an extraordinary 86 per cent of cases she succeeds. There are some foreign physiotherapists who say it's all too much for the children, and that when they leave the embrace of the Institute and of Hungary they are unable to cope with the harsher realities of ordinary life and of more conventional treatment. Dr Hari is unperturbed. Her new institute will cost the equivalent of 120 million pounds - and she now has eighteen British girls taking the full four-year course to learn the techniques of conductive education.

In Birmingham in the British Midlands, a Peto-style Institute has been operating now for nearly three years. The day is coming when youngsters like Danielle will no longer need to take the trip to Budapest - although they'll miss a very special Hungarian experience.

Last March, East Germany went to the polls in the first free election the country had known. Reunification with the West followed soon afterwards on October 3rd.

THE LAST DAYS OF THE DDR

JAMES MORGAN   3 MARCH 1990

There was one statement I had been waiting all week to hear. It came at my final interview when the extremely agreeable man I was talking to said he had been a member of the Communist Party for years. But, he added, I knew nothing of the crimes of the leadership. He was almost old enough to have said this once before. I then recalled once reading a letter from a British ambassador in East Berlin who, on seeing a queue of old women in black, wondered if there had ever been another group of people who had known such an amazing variety of awful governments. The Kaiser's Reich and the war it connived at, the Weimar Republic and its inflation and unemployment, then Hitler and finally the so-called German Democratic Republic.

The probability, though, is that most of the old women in black didn't know they were living under awful governments - in fact they may have thought some of them were rather wonderful. The imminent demise of the German Democratic Republic has started a minor movement in East Germany where some people, particularly intellectuals, are looking for what was good about their state. Even the man in the street is wondering whether anything he values might be lost in the drive towards unity which will in effect be the unity of the cat and the mouse. For most people, being swallowed up is the only desirable outcome of the whole process of change in East Germany, but for many there is a hankering after the somewhat dimly perceived 'social achievements' of the GDR. These largely mean a guaranteed job for life but also imply what many call social solidarity. Wasn't this in fact, I asked one academic, the solidarity of the prison camp? He largely agreed.

The election itself is fought against the background of bewilderment about what the future holds and about what the different parties stand for. A free election is almost incomprehensible to the citizens of East Germany, and even more so when the parties are imported, sent fully grown and developed into a country where the vagueries of democratic politics are unknown. A cartoon in an East Berlin paper summed it up: a sweating politician shouts to a crowd, "What on earth shall I promise you now for God's sake?"

The West German politicians who barge about the country for a day or two are, it's widely recognised, fighting their own campaigns in the West. So in the end it is not surprising that half the electorate doesn't know how to vote and those who do hold their opinions lightly. Yet a paradox is that although public controversy is rare, ill-feeling runs high. Local politicians make hesitant statements about what they think, but take little notice of what others say. Their supporters meanwhile deface rival posters.

Whatever the result of the election, it is clear that it has helped create enough fear and resentment, on both sides of the border, to ensure that the path to unification, although inexorable, will prove a thorny one. The 'Wessies', as the East Germans call their brothers, are seen as high-handed, greedy and interested only in getting their hands on the assets of the East at the lowest possible price. Westerners portray the other Germany as a bankrupt slum that will eat up their taxes and threaten the stability of the widely-worshipped Deutschmark.

It's an argument where both sides are possibly right. When the next all-German government emerges it will undoubtedly be the product of the old Federal Republic. But the difficulties that could emerge - unemployment in the East, inflation in the West - will ensure that the so-called Democratic Republic lives on in some warped and ghostly form.

Maybe a few of the old ladies in black of East Berlin could live long enough to enjoy the unique possibility of living in a united, democratic, efficient and prosperous Germany. And maybe there will never be another generation of Germans who will tell the world that they hadn't known what was going on.

Two nations which suffered grievously from Soviet suppression - Hungary where Soviet tanks crushed its 1956 Revolution, and Czechoslovakia whose 1968 Prague Spring Reforms were brutally snuffed out by Soviet-led invasion - are now seeing the Soviet soldiers leave under new agreements.

THE RED ARMY GOES HOME

HAROLD BRILEY   BUDAPEST   10 MARCH 1990

As the Red Army began its biggest retreat since Hitler's hordes unleashed their 1941 Soviet invasion, it was not a bugle call for freedom which signalled Hungary's new era but the clank of a train taking the first three hundred troops home from Hajmaster station, 150 kilometres south west of Budapest, as a Soviet military band played on the platform.

The band's repertoire reached its climax with the Communist anthem, the Internationale, and the Soviet national anthem. But, for those Hungarians present, only their national anthem could reflect their true feelings.

For them, it symbolised the beginning of the end of the Soviet military presence since the Red Army vanquished the German army here in 1945 and also Hungary's new-found freedom as it approached its first democratic elections in memory.

Hungarians spoke, with emotion, of feelings from the heart, as they put it, that they are waving farewell not just to Soviet troops and 45 years of monolithic communist rule but to several centuries of foreign influence and domination by the Turks, the Austrians, the Hapsburgs, the Germans and the Soviet Union. Now, they said, Hungarians can be Hungarians. Foreign observers sensed the fundamental change of atmosphere and themselves rejoiced. A Western army officer told me: "The Hungarians are showing just how happy they are to be free." And a much-travelled West German businessman declared: "What a wonderful country without communism."

Even the departing Soviet soldiers told me how happy they were to be going home, as a senior Soviet Commander told me, the Soviet soldiers leave with pride, their duty done. But, he added, the Red Army remained ready to meet any threat from wherever it came. The General's sentiments were heartily endorsed by the soldiers themselves as they climbed aboard the train.

Demonstrators from Hungary's Federation of Young Democrats waved posters demanding that the troops get out sooner than next year's June deadline. Many Hungarians say it took Soviet tanks only three days to crush the 1956 revolution. Why should it take so much longer to leave? Why couldn't they leave by air, by the River Danube, and by road, as well as by train? The practical difficulties of transporting so many troops - fifty thousand from Hungary and seventy thousand from Czechoslovakia - with at least another one hundred thousand families and civilian staff in each case, along with vast quantities of military supplies, ammunition, fuel, artillery, and thousands of vehicles and tanks, take time to surmount.

3,500 trains were needed, most of them converging onto an already congested rail junction on the Soviet frontier, called Chop, where they would have to switch onto different gauge tracks. Even so, there were hopes that the withdrawal could be speeded up.

Politicians and military commanders alike want Hungary to pursue a policy it's already embarked upon - to create a bridge between East and West by building relations with NATO's political though not military framework, and other Western organisations, such as the European Community, without quitting the Warsaw Pact, at least not yet, though they want it to be a political rather than a military organisation, which it has anyway, in practice, ceased to be.

*Political changes in Eastern Europe have opened up a vigorous debate in
the new democracies about the future direction of their economies. But
how easy will it be to convert sluggish, monopolist industries nurtured
under communism into capitalist enterprises?*

CZECHOSLOVAKIA REVERTS TO CAPITALISM

JAMES MORGAN   BRNO   25 MARCH 1990

T he second city of the Czech lands is Brno. It stands high above the
fertile farms of Southern Moravia and itself is dominated by the
cathedral of St Peter and St Paul. The cathedral has been recently renovated
and has a solid, almost Scottish feel about it. For the rest, Brno is not a city
that would delay the tourist for long. It hasn't had that role in Czech history.
Brno is the centre of the country's armaments industry and gave its name to
the ubiquitous Bren gun of the Second World War.

Czechoslovakia's armaments industry has a long history. Hitler needed it
to launch his attack on France. He gratefully walked into Brno after being
allowed to take much of Czechoslovakia by Britain and France, where there
are still historians who reckon it was all an act of wisdom if not actual
statesmanship.

Czech arms dealers have what is sometimes called a controversial record.
In what were known as the Chaco wars, between Paraguay and Bolivia in the
1930s, they sat in the two capitals in constant radio contact, to tell each other
what they had sold to one side in order that the other might order the same.

Today, the man who leads a party dedicated to out-and-out free market economics says the only industry he would keep in state hands would be armaments. But it was, of course, the state-owned armaments industry that delivered the explosive Semtex which got into the hands of the IRA. So it is one of those inevitable paradoxes of history that, as Czechoslovakia becomes a democracy at peace with its neighbours in a disarming world, the one industry that could make a major contribution towards overcoming the country's difficult foreign trade situation, as well as being a world leader, should be armaments.

The bland replies of the officials at the Foreign Trade Ministry are not reassuring. Our factories, they say, will be converted to peaceful purposes where the technology will be most useful. The problem encapsulates in a particularly harsh form that facing all the newly-emerging democracies of Eastern Europe: what do they do for their next trick? The largely peaceful destruction of communism has to be followed by new policies, and in Poland that has happened already, as the country's leaders strike out for the farther shores of free marketry. East Germany is handing its fate over to a fairy god-chancellor in the West, and the nations further south plainly have a lot of building on their hands.

But Czechoslovakia is the one country that, in the view of its inhabitants, was ruined by communism. By that they mean that the others never added up to much anyway, while Czechoslovakia was in the 20s and 30s an advanced industrial democracy. The industries are still there, but there is no agreement about what to do about them.

I went to the headquarters of the giant CKD works in Prague, where the boss was a veteran of the reforms of the Spring of 1968, still a socialist and convinced of the need for his enormous engineering firm to remain in the hands of the state. By keeping his ramshackle empire together, he reckoned he could become the dominant force in the European, if not world, tramcar industry.

The economists who in fact run the government are split between radicals and pragmatists. The pragmatists are genuinely worried about what the population will accept. Privatising everything may be the best theoretical solution, but the concept conveys curious images in a world that knows nothing of shares, new issues and pension funds. In Britain Sid was the fictitious private individual who had a flutter on a few privatised shares. The Czechoslovak version of Sid is a foreign capitalist in a top hat who owns the lot. Nevertheless there is another reaction. The man who runs the Free Market Party told me that many people wanted to know if he was a follower of Mrs Thatcher and Ronald Reagan. When he said yes, they said good - partly, I think, because ordinary people, as was shown in East Germany, will support politicians just because they are as far away from communism as possible.

In Czechoslovakia, change arouses complex emotions. You may think this isn't unusual, but in that country it usually is true that the more things change, the more they are the same. You can see that on emerging from the railway station in Brno, where there are the usual signs giving one the directions to neighbouring streets. The main one has been papered over to read: T.G. Masaryk Street. Masaryk was the father of the country's independence in 1919, when the street was first so named. Before that it had been Archduke Ferdinand Street, named after the assassinated nephew of the Austrian Emperor. In 1939 it became Hermann Goering Street. In 1945 it was Masaryk Street again. After the communist coup in 1948 it was Victory of Socialism Street. For six months in 1968 it was Masaryk Street; then for another 20 years Victory Street once more. The Czechs wonder if the old street signs are still around.

On 9th April 1989, Soviet tanks and troops brutally ended a peaceful pro-independence demonstration in the capital of the Republic of Georgia in the Soviet Caucasus. Twenty people were killed in the Soviet Army's crackdown, thousands more sought medical treatment for injuries and the effects of poison gas. One year on, the mass rallies to commemorate what is now regarded as a national tragedy attracted thousands of people.

GEORGIA'S TRAGIC ANNIVERSARY

BRIDGET KENDALL   TBILISI   9 APRIL 90

Tbilisi is full of surprises. "Be my guest," says every second taxi driver, waving away a foreigner's money in an expansive gesture of hospitality.

"Don't listen to Moscow's lies," warns an eminent writer, arguing that it is the Georgians, Stalin and his henchman Beria who are being blamed for all Communism's ills, to keep Russians and other nations guilt free.

At the Georgian Institute of Marxism and Leninism, a monstrous neo-classical building in the best totalitarian tradition, the black, red and white flag of Georgian independence flys defiantly from one of the top windows. For this is no longer just a party institute. It is now home to the Georgian Monarchists, the National Independence Movement and the Georgian Popular Front.

Compare Lithuania, where Moscow sent in armed paratroopers to guard the Institute of Marxism and Leninism when the local pro-Moscow Communists complained it was being taken over by non-Party people. In Georgia they didn't react at all. Or rather, perhaps, Moscow decided it would be wise to look the other way. Even when, two weeks ago, the frieze of workers of the world above the institute's door was splashed with paint, and one member of the international proletariat had his plaster nose and forehead chipped off after someone lobbed a brick, there was no official protest.

In Vilnius, no-one has dared take down the huge Lenin statue in the city centre. In Tbilisi, there is now a permanent - though decidedly sleepy - police guard on the main Lenin statue, ever since a group of activists decided in March to have a go at getting rid of it. But elsewhere in the republic some ten to fifteen town squares have lost their Lenin statues, so a local police chief told me, taken away for cleaning is the official explanation. But, he agreed with a grin, from now on the statues would be lined up to gather dust in government cellars.

The rules in Georgia have always been different from other Soviet republics and the current reasons are not hard to find. When hundreds of thousands of people poured into Tbilisi, rallying for a whole night and a day, to pile red tulips and carnations on the scene of last year's tragedy and to scatter the red flowers as a symbol and a protest along the main street, it was clear that last April's brutal show of force by the Soviet army not only succeeded in shocking the republic. It also left a smouldering resentment.

Almost all Georgians I met shared the same point of view, expressed with an alarming passion which sometimes verged on the unreasonable. That last year's crackdown was unjust, that Moscow and Mr Gorbachev could no longer be trusted, that reported clashes between Georgians and other ethnic minorities were all part of a deliberate attempt to destabilise the republic, and that the only course now open for the Georgian nation was to stand together to get back independence, after almost two hundred years of what they saw as Russian imperial rule.

Before last April, Georgians might have reminded you that Tbilisi, over its long history, had been invaded some forty times, and mostly by their Muslim neighbours, Persia, the Ottoman Empire, and by what's now their Soviet neighbour, Azerbajan. Georgians used to say they tolerated their Moscow masters because at least Russia was a Christian ally. For a small country surrounded by Muslims, that was an important consideration. But down in the Caucasus, alliances are beginning to change.

Thus last January, Soviet troops were sent into the Azerbajani capital Baku, again to break up with some considerable violence what amounted to a nationalist uprising. So last week there were bus-loads of Azerbajani sympathisers arriving in Tbilisi, commemorating not just April the ninth in Georgia, but January the twentieth in Baku as well.

A hundred thousand fists raised in unison at a protest rally doesn't mean that Georgia is about to follow Lithuania's example and declare its independence, even though the local parliament and party have already bowed to pressure from local opposition groups and announced that Georgia's incorporation into the Soviet Union in 1922 was unlawful. Opposition leaders in Georgia argue there is no point pretending Georgia is independent until the Red Army has gone.

If popular resentment against Moscow continues to draw Muslim Azeris and Christian Georgians together, the recent Soviet military crackdowns in the Caucasus could turn out to have been a bad miscalculation.

In the spring of 1988 an article espousing a return to Stalinism entitled "I cannot waive principles" was published in the newspaper SOVETSKAYA ROSSIYA. The author was a lecturer in physics at a Leningrad institute, Nina Andreeva. But many believed that her ideas were supported by senior conservative figures such as Politburo member Yegor Ligachov. Since this time, Mrs Andreeva has become the standard-bearer of the Stalinists, and was recently elected as President of the Yedinstvo, or 'Unity' organisation. Stephen Dalziel met Mrs Andreeva at her home near Leningrad, and found that the passion which sparked the article is still very much alive.

THE PRINCIPLES OF SOCIALISM

STEPHEN DALZIEL   LENINGRAD   15 MAY 1990

The town of Petrodvorets, 20 kilometres west of Leningrad, is famous for the palace built by Tsar Peter the Great, fashioned after the French palace of Versailles. But whilst the building is still standing - thanks to extensive renovation work carried out after it was badly damaged during the German occupation in the Second World War - Petrodvorets has not been noted for its famous inhabitants since the last tsar was deposed in 1917.

Until, that is, Nina Andreeva's article appeared in *Sovetskaya Rossiya* two years ago. The town's postal workers must have been amongst the first to notice the difference. Mrs Andreeva has received over 10,000 letters in response to her article, not only from various parts of the Soviet Union, but from all over the world. They are carefully filed by town, region or country, and take up half a bookshelf in one corner of the single room which serves as lounge, dining-room, study and bedroom for Mrs Andreeva and her husband, Vladimir Tryushin, a philosophy lecturer at Leningrad University.

The modest flat in which the couple live is just the first of many surprises that greet the visitor. Perhaps I should have been prepared for the second. Mrs Andreeva, a striking, dignified woman of 56, is, after all, a Russian, and Russians are renowned for their hospitality. A guest had come to her home, therefore food and drink had to be provided. Before I even started the interview, we sat around the table for three hours eating, drinking and discussing a wide variety of subjects, not least her famous article, "I cannot waive principles." The principles in question are, according to Mrs Andreeva, true Leninist ones, and the only Soviet leader to follow them after Lenin's death in 1924 was Stalin.

I t is obvious that on this subject Mrs Andreeva and her husband think as one. "Look at the state of Russia in 1917," they argued. "One third of the population of the capital alone was totally illiterate. You think that our flat is cramped, but then people lived in barrack blocks, with just one shelf of a bunk bed for a whole family." It was only thanks to socialism, they believe, that Russia was dragged out of this backward situation. What they fear now is that President Gorbachev's policy of perestroika is turning the clock back, paving the way for the development of an exploiting class once again in Russia, and that the values of Stalinism will be destroyed. Instead of a society where people help each other, Nina and Andreeva and her husband are afraid that selfishness will take over, a selfishness that is alien to the Russian character.

But surely, I asked, you don't want a return to the time of the thirties, when people lived in fear, and no-one trusted anyone? Mrs Andreeva was quick with her reply. "The only people who lived in fear were those who weren't wholly given over to building socialism." I tried a different tack. "But can you really forgive Stalin for his crimes against the people? After all, some historians now estimate that 40 million people were killed or imprisoned under Stalin." Mrs Andreeva's answer was simple: "Lies. There's no evidence to support these figures. Those historians who say this are just trying to make money on the back of anti-Stalin hysteria."

I left Nina Andreeva's flat after five and a half hours of lively, yet often frustrating, conversation, coupled with the warmth of true Russian hospitality. There is no doubt that she holds her beliefs with a blind faith which warrants respect. But reflecting on the horrors which Stalin imposed on the Soviet Union and the current economic crisis facing the country, I couldn't help feeling that those beliefs do not point the way ahead for a state which now wants to be governed by the rule of law.

The recent changes in Eastern Europe have led to the communists losing not only power but property, forced by the new governments to give back the buildings and churches that were taken into state hands. In Czechoslovakia, fresh claims are now being made on some of these buildings.

RECLAIMING PROPERTY IN CZECHOSLOVAKIA

MARY HOCKADAY   KOSICE   28 MAY 1990

Kosice is the regional capital of Eastern Slovakia, a beautiful area of fertile hills and plains. Sadly, some of the most charming valleys are spoilt by ugly, poisonous and inefficient factories and chemical plants built in the 1950s. Kosice was one of the first cities in Europe to receive a coat of arms, and has a graceful Gothic cathedral in the town square.

On a hill a little way out of the centre is a gleaming white building, known locally as the white house. Built only a couple of years ago as the regional party headquarters of a Communist Party now fallen on hard times, many of its rooms are empty. Deputy Mayor Judita Stovkova is charged with the task of finding a new use for it, and the other buildings whose ownership is now open to question. As discussion continues, the white house is something of a white elephant.

Back in the town centre there is an ornate 19th century house, called Jakob's Palace. Until recently it was the house of Socialist Ceremonies, from weddings to official functions. Now, various groups have applied for office space. One request came from the Orthodox Church, which in the Stalinist years was given all the churches of the suppressed Greek Catholic Church and is now being made to give them all back. Mrs Stovkova has been at the centre of bitter rows between the two churches. Her diplomatic solution to the Jakob's Palace problem was to offer the Orthodox Church rooms but at a rent she knew they would not be able to afford.

Whereas the number of Greek Catholics is quite large enough to fill its reclaimed churches in the town, there is another religious group which is pathetically small in relation to the property it can lay claim to. There are three synagogues in Kosice, including a grand turn-of-the-century edifice built for the several thousand Jews in the town at the time. Now each Saturday in a smaller synagogue - the community cannot afford to heat the larger one - 35 Jews gather. At festivals perhaps 60 or 70. Thousands were deported during the war and after the war the Communists kept much of their property. The secretary of today's tiny Kosice Jewish Association, Jan Adamec, is determined to reclaim and refurbish Jewish property. He has yet to hear from the authorities about his request. He didn't seem that surprised. Asked which of the burgeoning political parties he looks to to best protect Jewish interests, he said "none".

H is distrust of officials and politicians even in the new area is natural. He remembers pre-communist Slovakia as a protectorate of Nazi Germany, with a clerico-fascist government under Father Josef Tiso. Yet to other Slovaks, such as Father Jan Seman, an elderly Greek Catholic priest, Father Tiso was a guardian of the Catholic faith who, faced with the choice of collaboration or invasion, chose the lesser of the two evils. Many older Slovaks, though ashamed of the State's deportation of Jews, look back on those years as a time when Slovakia was a stable and independent state.

For younger Slovaks, it is a confusing time. One student told me she can hardly keep up. For years the Communists vilified Tiso. Now she hears people call him a martyr. She laughs at the occasional problems finding her way around her home town, now that streets are reverting to their pre-war names, and churches and offices are being reassigned, but says finding her way round her history is more troublesome. In legalising the redistribution of buildings, the government can resort to documents proving former possession. Redistributing political power in the elections depends in part on the less tangible heritage of history. No-one has yet invented ownership deeds to historical truth.

In July Vaclav Havel was re-elected as president of Czechoslovakia for another transitional period of two years. As normality returned to Czechoslovakia, its leaders no longer had the excuse of being new to politics or working in crisis. In recognition of this the president's office was re-organised.

COMPUTERISING THE CZECH PRESIDENCY

MARY HOCKADAY   PRAGUE   2 JULY 1990

When the victors in last winter's revolution finally got access to the president's rooms at the Prague castle, they found the offices stripped bare. Typewriters, clocks, files were all gone. So had the Russian computers. Not only did the assorted dissidents, artists and novice politicians have to learn how to run a country, they had to create an administrative system with which to do it.

Since May they have had some outside help, in the shape of an ebullient American who has taken on the task of preparing an information system for the president's office. At the end of one of the castle's long, red-carpeted corridor Charles Ross sits in a small office surrounded by computers. He's 38, his crinkly hair has a life of its own, and he grew up in the thick of Washington politics. Watching him work is enormously revealing about how far Czechoslovakia has to go to achieve its goal of competing with West European countries.

The system he is setting up must be sophisticated but simple to use. When a user turns their personal computer on, the screen reveals the

Czechoslovak flag and the words Office of President Vaclav Havel. Charles Ross, a true American, says "I want people to feel good about themselves when they switch on in the morning."

Users can prepare documents, keep directories of ministers and officials and communicate with each other, and eventually Ross hopes other offices and institutions. The office staff will at last be able to deal with the backlog of unanswered letters to the president. In the past six months he has received 50,000 letters. Half still have to be answered. They also have to be analysed. In a country without sophisticated opinion polls, these letters are a vital indicator of public feeling. The restless mind of Charles Ross is already working on software to help.

Another major task is to put onto computer all the new legislation. This will eventually be available on a public data network which Charles Ross's company is also preparing. A team of students and volunteers is typing them into the system. At the moment, what with paper shortages and lack of printing and photocopying facilities, it's very hard to find out what Czechoslovak law actually is. Computers offer one solution.

Charles Ross is of course not doing all this for love. The Czechoslovak government has not yet paid for the presidential office system but he is confident they will, one day. From the financial point of view it is the public data network which will bring the real financial rewards, and he expects his company to be working in Czechoslovakia for some time. He has made some extraordinary deals on behalf of Czechoslovakia, persuading American companies to give computers and software free, or at 'emergency disaster relief' prices - his argument, that the survivors of an earthquake or communism both deserve help.

His contacts in Washington have helped get round export controls on what should or should not be exported to Eastern Europe. He has even found a way round the haphazard power supply in Czechoslovakia - another American contact is providing an uninterrupted power supply at the castle so that when the chandeliers blow the whole computer system doesn't go down. All good public relations, and perhaps a lesson to the Czechs and Slovaks that red tape is there to be cut.

The presidential staff have a wider purpose too, beyond building a support system so they can work less than sixteen hours a day, seven days a week. They are desperate to create a professional image as quickly as possible, so that foreign governments and potential foreign investors will take them seriously. They know that the goodwill and interest in Czechoslovakia and its Velvet Revolution will fade, and they will then have to deal with the outside world on competent, professional terms. Computers at the castle won't be enough. The whole country needs an information revolution, a revolution in attitudes to work, to business, to bureaucracy. But the professionalisation of the president's office is a token of the determination in the Czechoslovak leadership to turn the country round.

Charles Ross's system will soon be up and running, and he'll be giving computer lessons to the castle staff. As for the president himself, "Oh, he's computer literate" says Ross. "Don't forget, he's a writer. He knows how to use a word processor."

In the.Communist bloc, Albania was always the odd one out. First pro-Chinese, then anti-everybody. But now there are signs that its people are catching the virus of democracy sweeping through Eastern Europe, as many Albanians succeed in finding refuge in the West.

A WALK WITH THE SIGURIMI

MALCOLM BRABANT   TIRANA   31 JULY 1990

I t had been 3 days and there hadn't been a sniff of dissent. The only people who'd talked - in immaculate English - had been supporters of the regime of President Ramiz Alia. Even the younger ones had approved of the shoot-to-kill policy against would-be escapees at the borders. There had to be someone who wanted to leave and who'd be brave enough to say so. After all, 6,000 had defied the Kalashnikovs of the security forces to reach the sanctuary of western embassies, and eventually, foreign soil. Western diplomats said they represented just a fraction of the true number of people wanting to say goodbye to Europe's most oppressive country.

Foreigners are instantly recognisable to ordinary Albanians and to the Sigurimi, the not-so-secret police who watch you, watch them, and are extremely interested in any contacts. It's impossible to hide so there's no alternative to the brazen approach. But mention the BBC, and peoples' fear becomes immediately apparent as they walk in a wide arc around you.

I sat on a wall at the edge of a park in Tirana containing Joseph Stalin's statue and hissed "do you speak English?" at every passer-by. "No," most of them replied, with perfect accents. After half an hour, a trendily dressed young man with sad eyes stopped and said yes, but, he whispered, it's too dangerous to talk here. Can I follow you? I asked. No, he said and walked off. Then he turned and gave a discreet wave of the hand. The hour that followed proved an incisive cameo of life in Albania.

I gave him two minutes start and trailed him leisurely through the park. He went up towards the main square, past the government compound containing offices and comparatively opulent houses and its cordon of armed soldiers and Sigurimi minders who make it a no-go area for ordinary Albanians. Maintaining a healthy distance between us, I occasionally checked over my shoulder to see whether anyone was following me following him.

There was one possible tail - a thick-set man with the tell-tale flared trousers of the Sigurimi. I turned round, turned the video camera on him and asked why he was following me. That seemed to do the trick. Meanwhile, the dissident was blending with the thousands of Albanians enjoying their Sunday promenade. If this was a country in crisis, the sound of laughter and the sight of happy faces disguised it well.

The dissident ducked into a shabby courtyard - but there were children playing and so privacy was impossible. He ducked out again, and headed towards the university. It's closed for the summer, but it's expected to be a centre of anti-government protest when it reopens in September.

Whoever built Tirana obviously wanted to make the crushing of student rebellion as easy as possible - there's a barracks right next to the campus. But the dissident ignored the university and carried on into the woods beyond. To the left was proof that the Albanian government is worried about the prospect of more anarchy from people trying to leave. There was a big camp of military tents to billet reinforcements who'd been drafted in from other parts of the country. The dissident walked up the hill to where the trees were thicker. At last, after half an hour and two miles, it was safe to walk together. Were we being followed? he asked. I thought it was clear, apart from two children behind us pushing a bike. That could be dangerous, he said. Even children in Albania are used as spies. We plunged deeper into the woods, past courting couples lying in the grass. There's no spare accommodation in Tirana - this was the only place where they could be alone. Eventually we found a spot that seemed remote enough.

His name was Ardi. He was an engineering student of Greek origin. He and four of his family wanted to emigrate to Greece. You can't imagine how bad life is here. If you say or even think the wrong thing, you can be punished, he said. Just at that moment a man with flared trousers approached, pushing a bicycle. Ardi put my sunglasses on and dropped his head. Was it the Sigurimi? No, he said, the man didn't have a jacket for the radio and the gun.

The conversation continued. He didn't believe President Alia would carry out the reforms he'd promised. It wasn't worth staying so he would try to get a passport and a visa from the Greeks. He wouldn't consider jumping the fence and asking for asylum. Nor would he risk slipping across the border. 160 people are estimated to have been shot dead this year alone attempting that feat. Ardi told of one soldier being shot by his officer for refusing to kill six escapees. The officer then shot them dead. Ardi had no intention of becoming a victim, and, cautious to the last, he decided that he'd told me enough. We wished each other luck, said goodbye, and left the woods by different routes.

The next day outside the Greek Embassy there were scores of people with the same plan as Ardi queuing for visas. Troops and police were on hand to stop them storming the compound. Just along the road, workmen were clearing debris from the German Embassy. Like the French and Italian Embassies, it remains closed. But diplomats fear there will be another occupation as soon as they reopen. One said the exodus earlier this year had forced the government to harden its attitude and he feared another dash by refugees could end in bloodshed. Another diplomat predicted a massacre that would compare with the one in Peking last year.

The general consensus is that violence is inevitable and the catalyst will be the reopening of the embassies or the university. All the diplomats are hoping that if it does come to the crunch, the government, the police, the army and the dreaded Sigurimi will exercise restraint. That's Ardi's hope as well.

The Bulgarian Parliament has at last managed to elect a new president -
Zhelyu Zhelev of the Union of Democratic Forces. The previous
incumbent - Petar Mladenov - resigned over a video tape which showed
him calling in tanks to control an anti-communist demonstration last
December. But the decision as to who should succeed him was a far from
simple one.

A NOVEL WAY OF CHOOSING A PRESIDENT

OWEN BENNETT-JONES   SOFIA   4 AUGUST 1990

B ulgaria must be one of very few countries where having done an interview for the BBC is considered a qualification for Presidential office. But when Bulgaria's members of Parliament asked Chadvar Kuryanov of the Bulgarian Socialist Party - the renamed Communist Party - to tell them why they should elect him as president, that's one of the aspects of his career which he chose to highlight.

"I've experience of the West," he said, "after all, I've been interviewed by the BBC." This was too much for the opposition MPs. "Who interviewed you?" they cried. Mr Kuryanov was ready for that one: "Jonathan," he responded with as much authority as he could muster.

There have been many farcical moments during Bulgaria's latest stab at parliamentary democracy. With oil supplies running out, rumours of incipient food rationing and a virtually unmanageable foreign debt, the parliament found itself unable to discuss any policy matters. Instead it was deadlocked in a discussion about who should be the country's next president. But having spent the last 40 years or so toeing the Party line, the parliament was ill-equipped to deal with the decision.

There was the day, for example, when the three main parties - the Socialists, the Union of Democratic Forces and the Agrarians - at last came up with their candidates for the presidency. The voting began. In the first round no-one achieved the necessary two-thirds majority. So far so good. All the journalists - indeed many of the MPs - presumed that before the next round of the voting the third-placed candidate would withdraw leaving a straight run-off between the two leading candidates. But not so. The MPs voted for the same three candidates - with virtually the same result. So what to do next? Well, the same again, of course, and again. So four times they voted for the same three people and no nearer a result.

After intensive inter-party negotiations a breakthrough was achieved. One candidate would withdraw. But not the least popular - on the contrary, the most popular, Chadva Kuryanov, of the Socialists. And then they all started to tumble. Victor Vulkov of the Agrarian party - despite the fact that he almost certainly would have won - announced that he was bowing out of the race. That left the field clear for Peter Dertliev of the Union of Democratic Forces and a man widely considered capable of commanding respect on all sides of the parliament. "But no," he said, "you've had the chance to elect me and you didn't take it: I too am withdrawing."

Another opposition candidate was proposed, but with commendable speed he withdrew on grounds of age before a vote could even be held. So nearly a month after the previous president had resigned and five rounds of voting later, the parliament was left with no candidate at all. Indeed, the bug of walking away from high office seemed contagious. The Interior Minister, frustrated by an Opposition demonstration outside the parliament building, announced his resignation. "What's more," he said, "if any of the guards here had a gun, I'd shoot myself." The Prime Minister also seemed unhappy. "Frankly," he told me, "I've had enough of politics - if the light were shone on someone younger, I wouldn't be too concerned."

But still there was no president. In the end, and perhaps unsurprisingly after such a series of mishaps, the Socialists used their parliamentary majority to vote for someone they didn't really want. The presidency fell to Mr Zhelyu

Zhelev, the leader of the opposition Union of Democratic Forces. With the UDF MPs threatening to boycott parliament unless he was elected, and with both the unions and opposition demonstrators becoming increasingly dissatisfied with the parliament's paralysis, the Socialists caved in and gave the opposition what it wanted.

All in all, it was a chaotic performance but ironically it might prove to have been the best possible start for the Bulgarian parliament. I say that because Bulgaria's new politicians have now been forced to talk to each other and to do something politicians all over the world find difficult to do - to make compromises.

Communism may have been abandoned in Poland's political and economic life, but its architectural legacy is less easy to eradicate.

STALIN'S PRESENT

DONALD ARMOUR   WARSAW   8 AUGUST 1990

Warsaw has a low skyline, which makes its classic, post-war landmark all the more glaring. This looms over the centre of the city, a mixture of Gothic cathedral, fairy-tale castle, and the Woolworth skyscraper in New York. Depending on your viewpoint, metaphorically speaking, it's either a lasting tribute to Polish-Soviet brotherhood, or it's an eyesore imposed on the Poles; a constant provocation with its ostentatious red star up there at the pinnacle. This is the Palace of Culture and Science, a present from Stalin. 26 years ago, when I first visited Warsaw, the Palace of Culture, 200 metres high, had an air of discreet menace about it.

Now in the age of post-Communism it has more the look of a neglected giant, his dignity impaired by swarms of irreverent Poles working the market stalls around his feet. Its base is four pavilions in grey stone, each three storeys high, sprawling out from each corner of the edifice like giant lions' paws. They contain theatres, cinemas, concert and congress halls, a museum of technology and even a swimming pool. The upper part houses several institutes of the Polish Academy of Sciences. The Russian restaurant today has all the vivacity of a funeral parlour, its gloomy interior accentuated by the muffled sound of corner conversation from the few remaining customers. Above all this the heavy grey tower of the central section goes up and up and up, floor after floor, the cathedral spire disappearing on occasion into low cloud.

How do the Poles like it? 26 years ago they told me blandly about Stalin's present, but the subtext was that it was a present inflicted on an unwilling beneficiary. In an ironic vote of thanks to Josef Stalin they nicknamed it St

Joseph's Cathedral and they said you could get the best view of Warsaw from the top, because that was the only place from where you couldn't see the Palace of Culture.

So what happens to it now? Enter one John Kowalczyk, American entrepreneur of Polish extraction. Mr Kowalczyk wants to buy Stalin's present and turn it into an American-style trade centre. Irony of ironies - or is it? Warsaw's Palace of Culture was modelled on Moscow State University, but that in turn was inspired by early American skyscrapers such as the Woolworth Building. So if an American turns it into a trade centre, the Palace of Culture, this model of newthink, goes back to its cultural roots - if you see what I mean.

Mr Kowalczyk wants to make this anachronism more contemporary looking, so he will have to remove the innumerable folderols that adorn the balconies and the buttresses and get rid of the burly statues to heroes of labour in the wide open spaces around the Palace. Some Warsawite has already unofficially removed a vital part from one of these heroes in stone. But no matter how he cleans it up, the American businessman won't be able to take away the essential grey gloom of the Palace of Culture.

The Palace now has a new competitor just across the road. This is the American-built Marriott Hotel. In contrast to the gloomy tower of totalitarianism, the new Marriott Hotel represents a citadel of capitalism, a shimmering, glass-clad shoe box aimed at the sky; beside it the Palace of Culture looks distinctly un-shimmering, a reminder to any Soviet guest in Warsaw of what was, but is no more.

Poles are being less punctilious about preserving other monuments that Stalin left behind. Various local authorities are planning to demolish Soviet war memorials. Warsaw citizens still remember the uprising of 1944, when Stalin did not exactly rush to the aid of the Poles. Soviet troops stayed on the other bank of the River Vistula and didn't move to help the heroic but hopeless Polish Resistance. Every Pole believes it was because Stalin would not support a resistance that he didn't dominate. On that opposite bank of the Vistula, I found another monument - to Soviet troops. Unofficially, the Poles call it the Tomb of the Unknown Soviet Observer.

The fall of the Berlin Wall - perhaps the event of 1989 - was rejoiced about all round the world. The confrontation of the cold war was finally over; a people cruelly divided by concrete and barbed wire reunited. But the events of the past year have left many Berliners themselves with mixed feelings.

MIXED FEELINGS IN BERLIN

BEN BRADSHAW   BERLIN   16 AUGUST 1990

G o into any bar or shop in West Berlin, travel on any bus or underground train, the refrain you'll overhear is becoming an ever more familiar one: give us the wall back and preferably twice as high. Most of the people expressing this desire will admit under closer questioning that of course they're pleased about what's happened, but the bar stool or Berlin omnibus chat, reflects the genuine view held by many West Berliners that they've lost more than they've gained by the fall of their famous wall.

For decades West Berliners led a charmed existence; no commuters, no traffic jams, always somewhere to park. Fighting their way on to the underground or having to wait for a table at their local restaurant were things outside their experience. Huge subsidies from Bonn meant low rents and cheap and abundant culture - both high and low. The only disadvantage of being a West Berliner was that you were restricted to West Berlin, or faced the three-hour drive along the transit motorway to West Germany. But even that didn't bother most people, and one look at the map will show you why. Few cities in the world can boast such a huge expanse of forests and lakes. The level of boat ownership here is higher than in the maritime cities of Hamburg or Kiel. How many city-based foreign correspondents have, as I do, wild boar roaming at the bottom of the garden?

It used to take me between ten minutes and half an hour, depending on the time of day, to drive from the BBC offices in the centre of West Berlin via Checkpoint Charlie to the centre of East Berlin. If West Berlin traffic was relatively light, East Berlin streets were positively empty. Now the same journey along a shorter route thanks to the breaching of the wall can take well over an hour, and when you get there there's nowhere to park. I have now followed the example of a growing number of West Berliners and, with my tape recorder and microphone in a rucksack on my back, have abandoned the car in favour of the office bike. The trouble is that most East Germans are not yet ready for such practical or environmental considerations. They'd rather sit in a traffic jam in their second-hand West German car, enjoying the newly-installed stereo system at full blast, although it would be quicker to walk.

In West Germany there are 43.6 cars for every hundred people. In West Berlin the figure is 33; and in East Berlin less than half the West German level - 22 cars per hundred people. But, armed with their new Deutschmarks, East Germans are doing their best to catch up. The number of new car registrations in East Berlin used to run at around 17,000 a year - it's now nearly 1,000 a day. The number of cars within Berlin as a whole is expected to double within the next 20 years to more than 3 million.

It is not just the Berliners who are creating the congestion. Since the opening of the borders the city has re-established its traditional role as the destination for thousands of Central and Eastern Europe's poor and dispossessed. On any one day an estimated 100,000 Poles make the 50 mile trip for shopping. A joke currently circulating here goes like this: what are the first 3 words a Polish baby learns? Answer: Mummy, Daddy and Aldi - Aldi being the cheap West German chain store before which queues of Poles form every morning well before opening time. Several thousand Gypsies have arrived from Romania and Bulgaria. Many of them are encamped in the sedate Tiergarden Park in the shadow of the imposing old German parliament building, or Reichstag. Most appear to survive by begging, another big city phenomenon new to Berliners.

The influx has been accompanied by a surge in the crime rate. In East Berlin 75% of detected shop theft is being committed by foreigners. The number of robberies has more than doubled and police say more of the victims are being beaten up now as well as robbed. Big city aggression has become evident behind the wheel too. There were 50% more road accidents in East Berlin in the first half of this year compared with the same period in 1989. Drugs dealers are said to be having a whale of a time exploiting the previously untapped East German market. The East Berlin newspaper Berliner Zeitung asks forlornly in an editorial: Is this the price we have to pay for our freedom? For West Berliners it's the price they're paying for the end of decades of glorious isolation. If and when Berlin becomes the capital it will get much worse. Experts expect the current population of around 3 million to grow by 60,000 a year and to more than double within 20 years. If that happens, Berliners will have to get used to the quality of life endured by most big city dwellers of today: crime, traffic jams, overcrowded public transport, smog and queues - and not just outside Aldi.

*After three years as a student and journalist in Brezhnev's Russia of the
1970's - the Era of Stagnation as it has been dubbed - Mark Brayne
returned in September and detected a feel of change in the air.*

THE KILL OR CURE OF GLASNOST

MARK BRAYNE   MOSCOW   21 SEPTEMBER 1990

After the Bush-Gorbachev summit in Helsinki, there was something reassuring about the slow Soviet night train south across the flatness of north-west Russia to Moscow. On board the *Leo Tolstoy* was the familiar world of yesterday. A plate on the steps up from the lower platform proclaimed this to be a quality carriage built in the German Democratic Republic. Inside, there was a samovar at the end of the corridor, and the stern but motherly carriage attendant, with her array of silver teeth, dispensing rock-hard sugar cubes with traditional Russian tea in silver glass-holders. These were decorated with the standard issue pictures of the Kremlin towers, and of sputniks boldly circulating the globe.

As the *Leo Tolstoy* crawled slowly towards Moscow the following morning, this too was a land I remembered from the days of Brezhnev 20 years ago. The long ELECTRICHKA platforms of the suburban railway stations, the dilapidated wooden dachas of the city elite, the waterlogged quiet of the silver birch forests, where I would join my Russian friends hunting for mushrooms or taking long frozen cross-country ski tours. And everywhere still too the mess, mud and neglect of an unchanged Russian countryside.

But if Moscow appears unchanged, it is only on the surface. As I was embraced by the chaos, filth and noise of the capital, my taxi-driver from the

Leningrad station turned out to be a private entrepreneur with one of Moscow's hundreds of new co-operatives. He plunged into a political discourse which in my day would have landed him in labour camp for anti-soviet agitation: Mr Gorbachev talked too much and had lost all credibility; there was nothing in the shops and the country was falling apart. Maybe - his hands strayed worryingly from the wheel of his clapped-out Moskvitch - maybe there was hope for Yeltsin, the Russian president. But whatever happened, he'd had communism up to here. What Russia needed - and this is a refrain that echoed through every discussion in the days that followed - was a firm hand who would get the country back to work again. Who might he have in mind? Well, Peter the Great was such a man. So was Josef Vissarionovitch, also known as Stalin. And, my driver volunteered, Hitler may have been a *negodyai,* a good-for-nothing, but at least under him there was order.

A s I later made the rounds of my old liberal friends, I heard a very different, more tolerant recipe for resolving the agony of the Soviet Empire. Privatise the economy, open the floodgates to western investment, above all, let the republics go. But the analysis offered around the Russian kitchen tables where together we used to listen through the jamming to the BBC and Voice of America broadcasts was of a daily life incomparably more difficult than evening the austere days of Brezhnev. My friends, some Jewish, some Russian, spoke of possible civil war, of extremism and intolerance, of the distant rumble of fascism of the kind that rolled through the economically troubled Europe of the 1930's.

It sounds terrifying - but curiously, and for the first time since I fell in love with Russia as a student, I sensed just a little cause for hope. At a new open-air free market set in the Russian mud around a sports stadium in north-east Moscow, I found hundreds of private traders selling goods of a quality I had never seen before in Russia. There were scurrilous nesting dolls depicting leaders from Gorbachev through Stalin back to Lenin and beyond. There were paintings, carvings, crystal, and badges of the satirical kind that swept Solidarity's Poland ten years ago. These declared: I'm an Agent of the KGB, or I'm a Child of Stagnation. Police occasionally intervened - but a hundred-rouble kickback, and the trader was soon back in business. The rouble is virtually worthless; dollars and Marlboro cigarettes have taken over.

But it is now possible to stop a taxi on the street, and even to drop into a co-operative restaurant for a meal. There are the faint glimmerings of enterprise. Most important of all, the fog of fear, of the smothering conformity of the last 70 years, has finally lifted. It is difficult to exaggerate how important that is. The Russians, the Lithuanians, the Georgians and the rest are directly and fearlessly confronting their appalling past, and their present problems. The illness - communism itself - has at last been publically and ruthlessly identified. The fear now is that the cure will kill the patient.

WESTERN EUROPE

July	5 1990	NATO Summit in London
July	8 1990	West Germany wins World Cup in Rome
September	29 1900	Belfast Protestants mark 300th Anniversary of the Protestant Victory over Catholics at The Battle of the Boyne

The Twelfth of July 1990 was the 300th anniversary of the Battle of the Boyne, when the Protestant William of Orange defeated the Roman Catholic King James II at the Battle of the Boyne. The celebrations threatened to antagonise relations further between the communities of the divided city.

JULY THE TWELFTH IN BELFAST

CATHERINE UTLEY   BELFAST   12 JULY 1990

Waking up in my hotel in the centre of Belfast on the twelfth of July to the sound of the silver bands and the relentless beating of the drums, I am filled with a sense of resignation. I have been here before on the Twelfth and know that this music will be impossible to ignore. Wherever I choose to go, it will be there, dominating the day - never more so than on this 300th anniversary when the parades will be bigger and louder than ever. There is nothing for it but to go out and watch.

For the one hundred thousand or so members of the Orange Order - set up to commemorate the victory of the Protestant William of Orange over the Catholic forces of King James II at the Battle of the Boyne - the day has immense historical significance. For them, the Boyne meant the consolidation of the Protestant faith in Ireland and for many of those marching the fight for civil and religious liberties continues.

Three hundred years after the Boyne, Orangemen believe that their Protestant identity is still under threat and they cite as evidence the Anglo-Irish agreement which gives the overwhelmingly Catholic Republic of Ireland a say in the affairs of the north.

For most of those who take part in the Twelfth, then, it is a day of celebrating their Protestant heritage, and also very much about having a good day out. Robert Martin is a new recruit to the Orange Order. He is also a member of the Gold Springs True Defenders in Comber, outside Belfast, which leads his Orange Lodge at the Twelfth parade. This is a blood-and-thunder band of flutes, drums and cymbals, played as loudly as possible - also known as a 'kick the Pope' band, but Robert Martin disputes any suggestion that it's triumphalistic.

•

any of Northern Ireland's half a million Roman Catholics - the minority one-third of the population - are offended by the Twelfth of July, particularly those who live along the routes of the parades. In Portadown, to the west of Belfast, Catholics are angry that Orangemen insist on parading past their homes every year. For Catholics, the memory of King William's victory at the Boyne is no cause for celebration. The political historian, Dr Eamonn Phoenix, argues that the historical significance of 1690 for them is very different from the Protestants: "Whereas for Irish Protestants, the Boyne removed a threat and consolidated the Protestant ascendancy in Ireland, for Irish Catholics it amounted to defeat, to dispossession, to the ushering in of the era of the Penal Laws which lasted for over a century; which closed the professions to them; which prevented them from buying land; which, if you like, dashed all their hopes."

So where - to ask a question which has been asked many times before in relation to Irish affairs - will it all end? Both communities remain steeped in their history, each apparently determined not to see the other's point of view. The Northern Ireland Secretary, Mr Peter Brooke, is currently engaged in efforts to bring Catholic and Protestant political leaders together to try to work out a way of governing the province which would be acceptable to all. It's not until you have lived through the Twelfth of July and gone to bed with the drums still beating in your head, that you can understand fully the enormity of his task.

In July NATO leaders meeting in London published a new blue-print for peace to bury the Cold War, heal the division of Europe, and end the cycle of peace and conflict that has marked most of this century. The London Declaration, as it is called, joins other famous declarations which could change the course of history. Harold Briley, a veteran of many a previous NATO communique, looked behind the words of the Declaration to find out what they meant.

FROM MISSILES TO CHOCOLATE FUDGE

HAROLD BRILEY   LONDON   25 JULY 1990

The newspaper headline said it all: "NATO DECLARES PEACE ON THE WARSAW PACT". These were among the more sparkling of the torrent of words that poured forth from this NATO Summit. The wording of the Declaration came under the closest scrutiny. "Declaration", you'll notice, not "Communique." It's the difference between what regular NATO ministerial meetings and what Summits, more grandly, produce.

NATO harbours deep within its bosom a very special breed of wordsmiths whose task over the years has been to produce phrases that mean either nothing at all, or all things to all men or women. One woman, in particular, is meticulous in her microscopic analysis of what the words say and what they might mean - Margaret Thatcher, the host leader this time, made her mark as usual not as, she said, "a Cold War Warrior" - which she denies she is - but as one of the more cautious leaders determined not to be fooled by the euphoria. For her, amongst all this talk of getting rid of nuclear weapons, there had to be retention of some of the old phraseology to preserve the purity of the nuclear deterrent.

So there it was: "The Alliance must maintain for the foreseeable future" - UNforeseeable might be a better word - "an appropriate mix of nuclear and conventional forces ... There are no circumstances in which nuclear retaliation in response to military action might be discounted." Ah, but wait a moment, the next sentence says something different, doesn't it? It's George Bush's now favourite phrase, declaring nuclear weapons to be truly a "last resort." In another famous phrase, the strategy of "flexible response" is to be modified to reduce reliance on nuclear weapons. Hold on. Hold on. I need an interpreter. "What's it all mean?" I asked a direct, no-nonsense military man. "Simple," he said. "It makes no difference. They've always been weapons of last resort. We're telling the Russians 'We're keeping our nuclear weapons - and you still won't know when we'd use them'." A Foreign Office man explained, in diplomatic double-talk: "The nuclear deterrent retains its deliberate ambiguity."

The wordsmiths triumph again. Ah, here's George Bush himself, smiling away, beaming peace all over the place, holding out the hand of friendship, telling everyone: "The East are no longer our adversaries." And who's that man just behind him? He's always with him. Yes, of course. He's the guy - a naval commander this time - who carries the instant high-tech communication equipment for the president to send the coded signal to launch nuclear weapons against the Soviet Union if need be. The outstretched hand AND the iron fist. All those nuclear weapons, thousands of them - on land, in submarines, in the air, are still targeted on the Soviet Union ... just in case. And vice-versa. But, it's the spirit and the tone that matters. President Bush and Chancellor Kohl emerged, the true authors of the Declaration, the bridge-builders to the East, the pace-makers for peace. Mr Gorbachev, beset by enemies at home, is being thrown a lifeline by his former enemies abroad. He and other Eastern European leaders will cross the bridge to be welcome guests at NATO. NATO's Secretary-General Manfred Woerner and Chancellor Kohl are going to Moscow. Others will follow.

The German army - East and West - is to be combined and cut in half. Soviet forces are going home ... from Hungary, Czechoslovakia, and elsewhere. The trains are cluttered up and clattering East with soldiery and military impedimenta, and will be for years to come. Demobilised soldiers are searching for jobs and for a place to live all over the Soviet Union. As the armies contract, the new growth industries are the peace observers verifying arms agreements and war-surplus scrap metal. The British, who invented the tank, are working on cheap, simple ways of destroying them. In a modern version of the biblical swords-into-ploughshares routine, the Russians talk about turning tanks into tractors. And, nuclear missile plants into factories making ... chocolate fudge. Yes, I did say, chocolate fudge. "That's hard to swallow," one NATO General said to me. "Hope I never have to eat the fudge." A hard-line Communist General of my acquaintance in Eastern Europe, who'd spent his life indoctrinating recruits with Communism and preaching the Cold War, told me what it now all meant to him and I think got it just about right. "I'm going to retire," he said, "go fishing, and play with my grandchildren."

Italy has called an official halt to the growing number of Third World migrants entering the country in search of work. From July any non-EEC citizen without a resident's permit faced deportation. Many Italians have been expressing fears that their country may soon be swamped with economic refugees from Africa and Asia.

ITALY'S UNINVITED GUESTS

DAVID WILLEY   ROME   26 JULY 1990

The tell-tale signs of growing intolerance are plain to anyone seeing the rough treatment that some African street vendors receive, both from the public and from the police.

One uptight school teacher who asked her class to open the windows to remove the smell when some East African students joined her course was sacked, although not without some protests by her colleagues. Owners of seaside villas and apartments arriving to open them up for the summer holidays have been finding uninvited North African guests in residence and calling in the police. Italy's biggest circulation newspaper wrote of seaside squatter incident: "to say that sooner or later the blacks are going to occupy our homes is no longer a commonplace, it's actually happened".

Until now practically all foreigners could enter without visas as tourists. The police asked no awkward questions about means of support. But under pressure from Community members who fear that Italy might be used as the developing world's back door into Northern Europe, intending migrants have to satisfy more stringent requirements. There is even a new proposal for health testing after a recent cholera scare in Naples and AIDS statistics which put Italy high on the epidemic's international casualty list.

Italy has five thousand miles of Mediterranean coastline and mountain frontiers to patrol, if the government really wants to control immigration. There is no coastguard service. The army and navy are to be called in to help the border police. The soft points of entry are the frontier with Yugoslavia, the Straits of Messina and the Bay of Naples. With well over a hundred million foreigners entering and leaving Italy legally each year, the task of checking new arrivals is not easy. The problem isn't just preventing further illegal migration but finding out just how many refugees from Third World poverty are already being provided with shelter. Latest estimates say over a million, although the official figure is only a quarter of that.

The Italian government doesn't want to shut the door on those in need, but it cannot yet offer or even afford the public welfare services needed by immigrant workers. The spendthrift Italian welfare state offers notoriously inadequate arrangements in health, education and social security, even for its own people. It was announced in July that interest on Italy's public debt has now reached the equivalent of the entire gross national product.

A worse problem is the extent to which organised crime has already formed a way of using cheap foreign labour for drug peddling and prostitution. The Naples mafia had to use its traditional method of murder by masked gunmen to show who the bosses really are when black Africans tried to muscle-in on the heroin and cocaine market. Five Africans were killed and seven people seriously injured last April when a bar in Caserta was raked with machine gun fire in a local settling of accounts by drug barons. Nearby, tens of thousands of African live and sleep rough as they earn starvation wages as pickers in the tomato fields. They have no incentive to follow the advice of the authorities and get proper working papers and residents' permits. They know that employers, who are also under local mafia control, will never pay social security contributions while there is a surplus of cheap African labour crying out for work.

But many ordinary Italians, mindful of their own experiences and that of their families as overseas migrants escaping poverty here at home, remember what it's like to be living in a strange country without a job or friends. They've held out a helping hand to the new arrivals: after all, a country which exported over twenty five million of its own citizens during the last century cannot really grumble about returning a bit of hospitality.

*At the end of July British members of Parliament embarked on their long
summer break, not to return until mid-October. At the end of the
Parliamentary year, Andrew Whitehead gave us a flavour of what it is like
to work at Westminster.*

WORKING AT
WESTMINSTER

ANDREW WHITEHEAD   LONDON   27 JULY 90

I work in a place called "The Dungeon". A small room with latticed
windows down a narrow stone spiral staircase. As Commons offices go,
it is a little on the small side. Perhaps ten feet by eight. Two of us work there.
And there's radio equipment, two tape machines and three computer
terminals.

When I tell members of Parliament how cramped the place is, I don't get
a lot of sympathy. Honoured are the MPs who have an office to themselves.
Some are squeezed three to a room in temporary buildings installed on the
roof. Even less fortunate are those in the "Cloisters", a bit like a dingy
teacher's common room. Rows of desks, with little space and no privacy.

It's not just the office facilities which are a little antiquated. In the
Members' cloakroom there's a ribbon on every coat-hook. That's where you
hang your sword. The House of Commons doesn't actually get going until
half-past two in the afternoon. It's assumed that most MPs have outside jobs.
The main evening votes usually come at ten or after. And, yes, most MPs are
expected to stay. Not in the Chamber listening to the debate. By mid-evening
there are rarely more than thirty MPs in their places. Perhaps they're in their
offices - if they have one - answering constituents' letters, or in one of the
bars or restaurants whiling away the time until the division bell rings. The
voting is not some sophisticated press-button system. MPs have to be

counted through the "ayes" lobby or the "noes" lobby. It can take up to a quarter of an hour.

All this hanging around encourages what is the main pastime at Westminster; gossip. In the alcoves, the corridors, the tea rooms, the lifts - anywhere two people can pass on news of others' indiscretions. The whole place buzzes with intrigue. And there's no place quite so intriguing as the Members' Lobby. This is the area where MPs congregate as they enter and leave the Commons Chamber. And here that privileged beast among Parliamentary journalists, the lobby correspondent, can loiter, accumulating gobbets of information and opinion.

Any conversation here is on 'lobby' terms. You can report what was said, but not who said it. No finger-prints. "The Cardinal rule of the Lobby", says the rule-book, "is never to identify the informant." As for briefings of the Lobby, the next page asserts: "Members are under an obligation to keep secret the fact that such meetings are held." And below in block capitals, we're warned: "Don't talk about lobby meetings before or after they're held."

That was written back in 1982, and since then things have relaxed a bit. I don't think I'll be excommunicated for telling you that twice a day - in the morning at Downing Street, and in the afternoon in a room high in a Commons tower - the Prime Minister's Press Secretary or his deputy gives off-the-record lobby briefings. Here we get the Prime Minister's eye-view of the political landscape. "A crutch for crippled journalists," says the political editor of one of three national newspapers which have withdrawn from the lobby system. It's not quite so sinister as is sometimes made out. But it can be uncomfortably cosy.

The other side of working at Westminster is sitting in the Press Gallery, looking down on the bear pit below, reporting what transpires. There's a great deal of theatre in the Commons. And now the television cameras are there, it's not just a matter of learning lines, but wardrobe and make-up as well.

The Commons, like the British court system, is adversarial. It's about combat not consensus. Government and opposition benches face each other. At Prime Minister's Question Time twice a week, Margaret Thatcher and Neil Kinnock are eyeball to eyeball. The front benches are two swords' lengths apart. It makes for great drama, great tension, great excitement. But great government? I'll leave that for you to judge.

Most people believe that economics is an intractable, depressing subject. The miserable science in fact. James Morgan has never believed it. When he took his family on holiday to Italy, he wanted to see how much he could understand about the way the Italian economy worked - just from watching what went on around him.

ITALY, WHERE THE ECONOMICS IS EASY

JAMES MORGAN   FLORENCE   20 AUGUST 1990

I t was a surprise to see them in the Basilica of San Domenico in the old Tuscan city of Arezzo. Underneath the dynamic frescoes of Piero della Francesca two surprisingly young women were offering the services of the oldest profession. It seemed a poor market. After all, the potential clientele was in small tour groups of earnest seekers-after Renaissance culture, or heavily encumbered by wives and children. And it was eleven in the morning. Nonetheless the spectacle did illustrate the entrepreneurial audacity that characterises the Italian approach, a willingness to take risks and find new market opportunities. After all, only an Italian car manufacturer would ever have thought of building a giant car plant on the River Volga, deep in Russia, in a purpose-built city named after Togliatti, a dead leader of the nation's communist party. Well, some might have thought of it, but only Fiat could have made it profitable.

Italy is among the more puzzling economies. It shouldn't really work, it often appears not to, but in some ways it is unrivalled. I have always believed that economic management, or the lack of it, is primarily a cultural phenomenon. The way people operate on the national scale reflects their private preferences and prejudices. The Italians have always had a reputation for superficial brilliance that hides a poverty-stricken reality. A British traveller in the sixteenth century called them a frippery of bankrupts. That was always nonsense. The powerful Venetian lust for cash, the saturnine brilliance of the Florentines in amassing it and the dominance of the Lombards in early European banking are all testimony to the solid materialism that is so evident to even the most casual tourist. When he fills up his petrol tank he will find it costs nearly twice as much as it might do at home, even if he uses the funny coupons so assiduously made unavailable by the authorities. This is because few people or companies pay much income tax - so the government has to get money somewhere. By not paying direct taxes, Italian enterprise isn't crippled in the north European way.

The money itself is only part of the burden. It's the bureaucracy and paperwork involved in preparing accurate accounts that makes life so difficult. Now you might ask, how on earth does the government pay its way in such circumstances? The answer is, of course, that it doesn't. Italy has a budget deficit in comparison with which the Federal deficit of the United States pales into insignificance. But isn't it terrible to have a huge budget deficit? Well, no - not if people save enough to lend to the government to cover it. And Italians save like mad. Another common illusion shattered. They save a lot, of course, because they don't pay income tax. But what is it that makes the economy work, if so much is unrecorded and untaxed? The answer came home to me while watching the evening crowds parade among the colonnades and piazzas of the northern industrial town of Reggio, in Emilia.

I recall how my father came home from Italy with a violent hatred of people who draped their cashmere coats over their shoulders and left dark glasses perched above their foreheads. In Reggio it was still the same story. The beautifully torn jeans, the finely-cut khaki thermal underwear that somehow appeared to be the height of fashion. The luminous, tight cyclists' shorts that left all too little to the imagination. The whole population was showing off, carrying stylish plastic carrier bags in the hope that others would believe there was more where that came from.

Now it is a commonplace of economic theory that a strong home market promotes exports. And of course, as everybody knows, it is design that makes Italy what it is. Everything is design in Italy, the principle of the bella figura which is supposed to illustrate the exhibitionism of the Italians is their great natural resource. It is an empty word, you can't think of anything when you think of design. But it's what gives the Italian economy its depth. That is why one has to look at the way economics actually work, as a cultural phenomenon. Italy possesses a solid economy, where progress can be measured and forecast with solid precision and which is but seldom blown off course. If you want volatility and febrile unpredictability you have to come to Britain.

After a week of huge celebrations in Berlin to mark German unification,
its citizens now have to adjust to everyday life. In the opinion of Ben
Bradshaw, many could be forgiven for thinking they still live worlds apart.

A TALE OF TWO CITIES

BEN BRADSHAW   BERLIN   6 OCTOBER 1990

I f an enterprising Berliner were to go into business supplying carrier pigeons, he or she would make a fortune. Although this is now the united capital of a united Germany it is still almost impossible to telephone from one side of the city to the other. The former East German authorities deliberately made communication between east and west difficult; not only did they allow just 7% of the population a telephone, but they arranged lines so that it was easier to dial Timbuktoo than West Berlin or Bonn. It still is, making a correspondent's life very difficult.

It must be even more tiresome for the business people trying to inject new life into what was the East German economy. The portable phone system is completely overloaded. One or two people I know in what was East Berlin have managed to get a coveted western line installed by claiming emergency reasons; but they should have kept quiet about it... they are now continually taking messages for other people and are suddenly the most popular guys in town.

The Wall has gone, as has the line on the map. Scores of roads connecting east and west have been reopened, as well as overground lines that have remained dormant since the Wall was built 29 years ago. But the average Berliner, emerging from his hangover after Tuesday night's celebrations, may well have thought he had imagined it all. It still costs twice as much to post a letter in what was West Berlin as it did in the East; car number plates from the West still begin with an "i", those from the East with a "b"; if you get into your car in what was West Berlin having drunk a couple of beers, woe betide you crossing the now non-existant border and getting caught. East Germany's total alcohol ban for drivers still applies in what is no longer East Germany.

The fact is that many of the laws that would standardise life between Germany's two former halves either haven't been agreed on yet, or would have been too risky politically to implement before December's all-German elections. Take the testing of motor vehicles for road worthiness: it has already started, but owners have until next March to get a certificate. That means six months' grace for the inimitable creation of the East German car industry, the Trabant.

T his spluttering little death trap on wheels falls down on virtually every EEC requirement, whether safety or pollution. But there are still more than three million of them on the roads, carrying the votes of three million families. Similarly, the peppercorn rents that applied in what was the East, and the minimal costs for electricity and solid fuel have all been frozen until the New Year.

The French and American commandants may have left amid flag-lowering and the bugling of the retreat, but everyone else is still here, still in their houses requisitioned at the end of the War, most of their costs still being paid by the German tax payer. One of the most popular of the 4,000 Allied laws that applied to Berlin exempted the people here from military service, which is compulsory in the rest of Germany. Logically, every male Berliner between the ages of 18 and 32 should now be getting his call-up papers. They are not, and it won't happen, if at all, until 1992.

Berlin still has separate local government in the former two halves, with separate services, and will have until December's elections. Public employees, be they teachers, nurses, dustmen or policemen who live in the eastern half, still earn on average a third of what their western counterparts do, although they may be treating the same patients, teaching the same children, collecting the same rubbish, or being showered with missiles by the same mob of anarchists.

Some things have changed - don't get me wrong. Taxi drivers can now

83

pick up passengers wherever they like. Until Wednesday, East Berlin taxis were only allowed to pick up in East Berlin, although they could drop down in West Berlin. The same applied the other way around for West Berlin taxis. This was a bit hard on East Berlin cabbies, because after currency union in July, prices rose so much that most East Berliners couldn't afford to go by taxi. But now, of course, there aren't any taxis left in what was East Berlin. And finding one that will take you there is like trying to get a cab to take you from the West End of London to the south of the river, after midnight, ten years ago.

Oh, and another thing has changed: former East Berliners who were lucky enough to have a job can't go shopping any more. West Germany's uniquely consumer-unfriendly trading laws dictate that all shops, hairdressers, and other providers of life's essentials are firmly shut by half past six during the week, and by midday on Saturdays.

THE MIDDLE EAST

March	15	1990	Iraqi execution of British Journalist, Bazoft, on Spy Charges
April	10, 22, 30	1990	Release of French and American Hostages from Lebanon
May	28	1990	Arab League Summit in Baghdad
June	21	1990	Iranian Earthquake: at least 20,000 killed
July	28	1990	Atatollah Rafsanjani wins Iranian Presidential Elections
August	2	1990	US Government sends Troops to Saudi Arabia
August	15	1990	Iraq accepts Division of disputed Shatt-Al-Arab Waterway with Iran
September	10	1990	Iraq re-establishes Diplomatic Relations with Iran
September	27	1990	Iran re-establishes Diplomatic Relations with Britain
October	8	1990	Israeli Troops kill 21 Palestinian Arabs in Jerusalem
October	13	1990	Syrian and Lebanese Troops defeat Rebel Lebanese Troops of General Aoun in Damascus.

The revolutionary changes in the Soviet Union and Eastern Europe are having an impact on the Middle East: the Arabs feel especially vulnerable to the loss of reliable support and are angered by the flood of Soviet Jews into Israel. Do the changes also have implications for the authoritarian Arab regimes themselves?

QUESTIONS ABOUT SYRIA

BARNABY MASON   QUNEITRA   10 APRIL 1990

T he day I went to Quneitra, spring flowers were blooming in the green fields, but a bitter cold wind blew out of Palestine. A torrential rain storm had eased off, and as the clouds thinned I peered through a telescope at the Israeli forces on the ring of hills around. One in particular bristled with electronics watching the plain below. Quneitra was destroyed by the Israelis before they pulled back in 1974; the Syrians have preserved the crumpled houses, the wrecked hospital, mosques and church like a museum, a reminder that their country will not be whole again until the Golan Heights - less than forty miles from Damascus - have been recovered.

In fact, President Hafez al-Assad doesn't see the changes in Eastern Europe as any reason for making concessions to Israel. He may have lost reliable allies; the Arabs can no longer play off one super-power against another; but that just emphasises the need for them to rely on their own resources, to act together. Why should we give up the aim of Arab strategic parity, officials in Damascus say, just when Mr Shamir - boosted by the Soviet Jews - is talking of a greater Israel?

The violent overthrow of President Ceausescu of Romania had a particular resonance in Damascus, since he was seen as one of Mr Assad's closest allies. The bloodstained body of the executed dictator was not shown on Syrian television, but in the days that followed a few graffiti briefly appeared on walls in the city: "Shamsescu, you're next" - Esh Sham is the Arabic name for Damascus. But nothing further happened; as one observer put it, Syria murmured, or rather whispered, but didn't move.

So when President Assad made a big speech to a youth congress in March, he argued that Syrians already had wide participation in government and a multi-party system - a reference to the six government-controlled parties grouped with the ruling Baath in the National Progressive Front. Mr Assad, unlike his young audience, still contrasts his regime with the more repressive government that he ousted in 1970. In 1982 a violent uprising by Islamic militants in the town of Hama was ruthlessly crushed, and many thousands died. The Muslim Brothers are still seen as a potential threat: if you give them freedom or let them form a party, one official said, they'd kill people and destroy everything.

Diplomats are convinced that any reforms will be cosmetic. The regime can't reform, one said; it's run by a minority - the Alawite community - and can't share power without losing it. He was equally sceptical about the chances of real liberalisation of the economy, since an elite group of military and intelligence chiefs are believed to profit from the workings of a vigorous black market which depends on an artificially high exchange rate.

Huge quantities of goods are brought in over the mountains from Lebanon while Syrian pounds are smuggled out by the lorry-load. The pounds are brought into by Lebanon or Jordan by Syrians working abroad, who thereby get a vastly better rate for their hard currency. The trade is fed by the fact that although it is illegal to take Syrian pounds out of the country, it is perfectly legal to bring any amount in.

A certain section of society has continued to thrive through the lean years of the eighties. I saw some of them at a lavish party in one of Damascus's five-star hotels. Girls in short skirts and bouffant hair-dos, boys in multi-coloured trainers eyeing them from the top of a spiral staircase. Nothing extraordinary in that, but a striking contrast to President Assad's own personal austerity and his message to Syrian youth: it is your great energies, he said, that are the guarantee of our revolutionary march.

Any Muslim country bordering on Iran could be suspected of being
vulnerable to Islamic fundamentalism. But people have always argued
that Turkey is a special case. It is a country with a strong secular tradition
and commitment to the West. But Turkey's brand of Islamic
fundamentalism is more creeping than revolutionary, but that doesn't
make it any less controversial.

ISLAMIC FUNDAMENTALISM IN TURKEY

JANE HOWARD   ANKARA   10 MAY 1990

The summer is hotting up here and Turkish women are showing off their legs in mini skirts that wouldn't look out of place in Paris or Rome. But alongside the teenagers in denims and Benetton T-shirts are girls wearing pale voluminous headscarfs and long drab raincoats, no matter what the weather. This is the sign of a devout Muslim, and it is becoming a more and more common sight.

A woman friend of mine told me in all seriousness that it is getting harder to wear a mini-skirt these days. That is certainly what a team of champion lambada dancers found recently, when the State-run television company requested them to abandon their frilly outfits and wear trousers to protect their modesty. The dancers refused, but compromised on black tights.

It may seem schizophrenic, but then Turkey is a paradox: a ninety-nine per cent Muslim country, but a secular state, where Islamic political parties are banned. The Turks are immensely proud of their secular traditions, which date back to the founder of the republic, Mustafa Kemal Ataturk. In a series of mind-boggling reforms in the twenties and thirties he abolished the Caliphate, which had made Istanbul the centre of the Islamic world. He brought in western-style dress, introduced the Latin alphabet rather than Arabic script, and did away with religious education. He is still a cult figure in Turkey today, but his face is no longer on the front of every child's school books.

Indeed, one of the main pieces of evidence to suggest that Turkey is becoming a more religious place is the boom in special religious schools. Religious education was made compulsory after the 1980 military coup. Some say that the armed forces, traditionally a bastion of secularism, may have seen religion as the opium of the people. Another indicator is the number of Turks who make the pilgrimage to Mecca each year. It has increased almost ten-fold over the last decade. Last year the government department responsible for religious affairs had its budget boosted by two hundred and thirty seven per cent.

The Westernised elite are battling against this creeping rise of Islam. A recent opinion poll listed Islamic fundamentalism as people's number one fear, above terrorism and inflation. Western diplomats constantly find themselves explaining why Turkey is not another Iran, despite being next-door neighbours. Firstly, they say, the Turks belong to the Sunni, rather than Shi'ite branch of Islam. Secondly, there is no influential network of clergy equivalent to the Mullahs in Iran. On the other hand, the conditions for a religious revival are there, with a massive population move from the villages to the cities, and the feeling of rootlessness which accompanies rapid urbanisation. There is endless speculation about whether Iran is trying to export its Islamic evolution over the border.

In fact there is more evidence of foreign intervention from the Saudi Arabians, who are Sunnis like the Turks. Journalists and academics have traced Saudi money being channelled into Islamic banks, charities and educational foundations. The younger brother of President Ozal is a consultant to one of these banks. Indeed, the Ozal family has played an ambivalent role in the rise of Islam. On the one hand they are western-educated and liberal in outlook, on the other hand they are devout and widely believed to be members of a powerful Islamic brotherhood, known as the Nakshibendis. The governing Motherland Party, founded by President Ozal, is a conglomerate of liberal, nationalistic and religious right-wingers.

About half of the present cabinet, however, are said to be religiously inclined.

There is a small party with religious leanings, the Welfare Party, which, by the way, was the only party to object to Turkey's application for membership of the European Community; and a fierce debate is now going on about whether the ban on fundamentalist parties should be lifted. But there seems to be more chance of the government lifting its ban on Communism than allowing an Islamic party.

One of the symbols of the fundamentalists' crusade is the great Byzantine cathedral of St. Sophia in Istanbul. Built when the city was the capital of the Christian world, it was turned into a mosque at the fall of Constantinople in the fifteenth century. Ataturk made it into a museum. It is dusty, dark and feels rather neglected. Outside is a cluster of people with a petition which they say carries more than a million signatures. They want to turn the magnificent building back into a mosque.

For two-and-a-half months in early 1990, Egypt saw the most serious outbreaks of violence against the minority Christian community for ten years. Rioters in rural Upper Egypt set fire to Coptic churches and shops, and attacked the Copts themselves. Much of the trouble was blamed on Islamic militants, but as Barnaby Mason discovered, that was too simple an explanation.

EGYPT'S CHRISTIANS & MUSLIMS

BARNABY MASON   SANURIS   14 MAY 1990

I n the village of Sanuris, about sixty miles south of Cairo, two lorry-loads of riot police guarded the Coptic church in case of trouble. A couple of days earlier crowds of boys and young men had gone on the rampage, smashing up Christian shops and badly injuring several people. The church of St. Michael itself, decorated with gaudy pictures of the archangel crushing the devil underfoot, escaped damage, but the perimeter wall had been heightened by six feet to stop local boys and breaking the windows.

The riot was sparked off by a rumour, to the effect that a Muslim girl had been raped, or even killed, by an elderly Christian grocer, and it continued despite efforts by the girl's father to show she was unharmed. A similar rumour had preceded a more serious outbreak of anti-Christian in the Minya area further south; there it was alleged, apparently without foundation, that the Coptic owners of a sweet factory had been sexually exploiting Muslim girls - either for pornographic videos or prostitution.

Egypt's Christian community is very ancient; the oldest monasteries in the world were founded in the Egyptian desert in the early fourth century, and it was here in a cave at the top of a mountain that St Anthony wrestled with temptation. In the towns and villages of the Nile valley, the minority Christian communities are interwoven with the Muslim majority.

Many names are Coptic: Sanuris means 'city of beauty'. The priest in Sanuris, Father Moussa Yohanna, puts the number of Christians there at ten thousand, about a sixth of the total. Almost certainly the proportion nationally is much lower, but there are no reliable figures; it is a sensitive subject for the authorities.

There are frequent clashes in Egypt between the security forces and Muslim militants campaigning for the introduction of an Islamic state. Generally they have been dealt with easily enough, usually by rounding up large numbers of the usual suspects. But as economic hardship bites deeper - the appeal of Islamic fundamentalism, a simple answer to a lot of complex questions, tends to strengthen too. One group of fifteen young men shot dead in the Fayoum area at the beginning of May had been attracted to their militant group partly by the offer of free food and lodging. But that doesn't explain why the militants' hostility should be turned against the Christians on a scale not seen since the beginning of the eighties.

One extremist group is accused of inciting hatred of the Christian minority by inflammatory sermons at Friday prayers. Father Moussa, full-bearded, shrewd eyes beneath his black hood, believes the militants attack the Christians in order to demonstrate that the authorities can't control the situation. Others argue that the militants see the Christians as part of the ungodly society which they want to overturn.

It is not the traditional Islamic view, which has generally accorded a measure of tolerance towards Christians and Jews. And most Egyptian Muslims are tolerant of their Coptic neighbours. Ordinary people of both religions flock to festivals commemorating holy men and women - saints' days in fact, though Islam is not supposed to have saints. And when the Virgin Mary was reported recently to have appeared in Port Said, miraculously removing a tumour from a woman suffering from breast cancer, Muslims as well as Christians were among the crowds who gathered around the church. That kind of deep-rooted co-existence is perhaps the best defence against bigotry and intolerance.

Arab leaders held a summit meeting in the Iraqi capital, Baghdad, at the
end of May that was summed up by one influential Arabic language
newspaper as "A summit of lowest common denominators." Many Arab
summits are like this, with consensus and compromise prevailing. But
usually there's one beneficiary, and in this case, it's widely argued, it was
the host - the Iraqi leader, Saddam Hussein.

THE MAN WHO WOULD BE KING

TIM LLEWELLYN   BAGHDAD   5 JUNE 1990

On the afternoon I visited the Tomb of the Unknown Soldier in Baghdad, I and a friend from the Guardian newspaper were the only people bothering to make the pilgrimage. Perhaps it was not surprising - it was noon on a work day; the temperature was nearly 120 degrees Fahrenheit and the nearest tree was a mile away.

Both here and at the Memorial of the Martyrs, where again no Iraqis were evident, two things became clear: that these war memorials in Iraq do not commemorate the dead, the wounded and the bereaved of the eight-year long Iran-Iraq War. They are million dollar, billion dollar tributes to the man who made the war possible, Saddam Hussein. The hands that clutch arched scimitars in soaring triumph at the Tomb of the Unknown Soldier were modelled on the hands of the President himself, and dangling from the haft of the swords are rope sacks, filled with the helmets of dead Iranian soldiers as if he collected them.

The vaulting ego of Saddam Hussein is a phenomenon that the Arabs in the outside world are finding it hard to cope with. His defiance to the world in general strikes a deep chord in Arab hearts inside Iraq and well beyond. Yet he has both overawed, impressed and terrified most of his own subjects.

One of the reasons few Iraqis visit the Tomb of the Unknown Soldier is that it is close to one of the many presidential palaces in and around Baghdad. If you take a wrong turning or break down near there, your car is seized and never seen again. The same could happen to you. The need to sustain such an ego can never be sated. The war memorials after all appear to suggest that it is Saddam Hussein himself who won the war, not the Iraqi soldiers. Generals and other senior officers who take public pride in their military successes are quickly cut down.

Since the end of the Iran-Iraq war, ordinary Iraqis have been looking in vain for some of the rewards that a nation seeks after it's sacrificed its sons, its brothers, its fathers, and many of its aspirations. What rewards there have been have gone largely to the fat cats who, in family, proximity or spirit, sit close to the president. The general public does not starve, but neither does it prosper, nor does it have much hope. In a country where few dare to speak to a foreigner - and most have been brainwashed to the point where even if they did speak they have little or nothing of worth to say - it is difficult to know whether resentment is breeding or not. This is not the point.

Saddam Hussein is frightened that resentment might be breeding. Paranoia builds daily. More and more of his extended family are being moved into security positions around him, some of them relatives who were unappreciated a few months ago. Private security firms have been hired. Saddam Hussein must be more than aware that at a party at the Officers Club in Baghdad last January, young army officers raised their mugs of Black Label whisky and shouted: "Thank you Ceaucescu!"

The Romanian dictator's demise, and the quick easing of various travel and economic restrictions that followed in Iraq were not just coincidences. Iraq, like all the other monolithic states in the Middle East, is well aware that the new freedoms of Eastern Europe and the Soviet Union have not gone unnoticed among its own people. After all, where now but in the Arab world is the decaying lexicon of Marxism still used to belabour the eyes and ears of the people - or should I say the masses, the strugglers?

Saddam Hussein has used his foreign policy, of which the Arab summit was one high point, as an antidote to such infections as democracy or self-expression, and raised the spectre of western threats and Israeli attacks to distract his population. The hanging of *The Observer* journalist Farzad Bazoft; the attempted importation of nuclear weapon trigger mechanisms; the 'supergun'; the threat of chemical weapons and worse - all these have been devices to bolster Iraq's fearsome image not so much abroad as inside the country itself; to emphasise to a people that might start asking questions that perhaps it is a little too early to be querulous when there is an enemy at the doorstep.

One irony in all this is that the United States, in the eyes of many observers of the Middle East, plays deftly into the hands of Saddam Hussein by its virtually unquestioning support for Israel and its hyper-reaction to an Arab leader who is much longer on menace to his own people that he is to the world in general. The United States and Saddam Hussein are, if you like, like two grinning undertakers shaking hands over a dying man - the downtrodden Arab.

The summit was a triumph for Saddam Hussein because he left his military threat hanging, stood out as the hero of Arabia, yet managed the conference in a careful and statesman-like way. The Palestinians pretended to go away happy because their cause was emphasised. King Hussein of Jordan was promised money and support. Saudi Arabia and Egypt limped home without major embarrassment for themselves and their friends in Washington. Syria stayed carefully and cautiously away. As a diplomat put it to me: "If the summit took anybody anywhere, it took President Hussein another step along the road towards preserving himself."

A decade after the Islamic revolution which brought down the regime of Shah Reza Pahlavi, Iran remains an enigma for the outside world. The leaders of Iran never seem to tire of singing the praises of the Islamic revolution, but visiting foreign journalists are looked at with suspicion or even hostility.

A DAY IN THE LIFE OF THE ISLAMIC REPUBLIC

JASVINDER SINGH   TEHERAN   12 JUNE 1990

Welcome to the Islamic Republic of Iran', says a poster under the watchful eyes of a huge picture of the late Ayatollah Khomeini. A stern-looking Khomeini is never very far from you in Iran. His photographs are everywhere; there are murals on the walls, posters hanging from buildings and trees, banners tied to lamp-posts, and framed pictures in government offices. The walls along the road from the airport have been painted with caricatures of the Iraqi leader, Saddam Hussein, carrying weapons, ordering his troops into battle or killing women and children with chemical weapons.

Most of this graffiti is old, with its paint peeling off the walls. But this macabre street art fails to evoke revolutionary fervour among Iranians any more. I asked one Iranian if he liked the colourful walls of his country. He shrugged his shoulders and said it was all propaganda for foreigners. In the capital, pictures of Khomeini and the defenders of the Islamic revolution go hand in hand. The security forces are everywhere. There are soldiers in khaki, policemen with walkie-talkies and, most feared and sometimes

96

respected, armed members of the Pasdars or Revolutionary Guards in green fatigues.

Pasdars are the true Islamic soldiers. Raised in the wake of the Islamic revolution, they may be asked to do the job of traffic wardens, normal policing duties or telling citizens whether their clothes are truly Islamic or not. They may stop a man for wearing a short-sleeved T-shirt and take him to the police station, or give him a lecture on Islamic decency. One schoolgirl told me how horrified she was when a group of Pasdars stopped her in the middle of a busy market place and told her that the top button of her shirt was undone. She nervously apologised; as she was not aware of it, they let her go.

Most women in Iran wear the 'hijab', a dress covering the entire body from head to toe. Only part of the face and hands are visible. Many young and educated women oppose these strict dress rules. The Interior Minister told us that the government does not force women to wear the hijab, but he spoke about the Islamic duty of women to cover - in his words - "those parts of the body which somehow affect men". Iranians have somehow become used to these vague dress codes and they go about their daily chores without giving them too much thought. Different variations of hijab can be seen on the university campuses and now even 'designer hijab' can be seen as well.

But the strict dress codes have not discouraged Iranian women from participating in everyday life. Women are to be seen everywhere - in government offices, in parliament, in shops, in bazaars and in the universities. Women are also outspoken and can be far more critical about prices and the bureaucracy. One middle-aged woman I met at a bus stop told me what she thought was wrong in the country; how public transport was being neglected, how files do not move in government offices unless you 'grease the palms' of officials, and much more.

Complaints about public transport, housing, shortages of meat and food are quite common. People say that the prices of everyday commodities have almost doubled in the past year. This is causing much hardship and many people are taking on extra work. Most common in Teheran is the use of private cars as taxis. Coupons for food and meat have led to black markets and hoarding. Many people say that drug addiction and prostitution are rising, but the government denies it. Government figures, however, reveal that over the past sixteen months, 50 tonnes of narcotics have been confiscated.

The fall in the price of the official currency, the rial, has led to an almost officially-sanctioned black market. Money-changers can be seen with wads of dollars, pounds and sacks of rials coaxing foreigners to change money. Newspapers regularly publish black market rates for the rial beside the official rates, one of the more exciting items of information in otherwise dull newspapers, which are dominated by reports of speeches by religious leaders. Newspapers carry long items about the opposition in Arab countries, but do not touch stories about Iran's own opposition. So Iranians get their news about the opposition from foreign radio stations, tuning in regularly to the BBC Persian Service, Israel Radio and the Voice of America.

In the middle-class homes of northern Teheran, people sipping illegally-brewed Armenian vodka and smoking American Winston cigarettes complain bitterly about the pariah status of their country. They also complain about the disappearance of nightlife in Tehran and how restaurants have to close early, although few observe these rules. But in the middle of their moanings, as their children listen to the latest tape by Michael Jackson or Madonna in their bedrooms, they also remind you that things have changed over the past few years. They say the mullahs are not so strict any more.

Saudi Arabia has long been an enigma to the outside world: an economic giant through its oil wealth, but using its political influence in the Arab world so discreetly as to be almost invisible; embracing consumerism but seeking until now to shun the social and cultural values of the West. Barnaby Mason gives his impressions from a visit he made before the Iraqi invasion of Kuwait.

GOD & MAMMON IN SAUDI ARABIA

BARNABY MASON   KUWAIT   18 JUNE 1990

Let me quote you something from the Old Testament - the first Book of Kings, Chapter 10, verses 14 and 15:

"Now the weight of gold that came to Solomon in one year was six hundred, three score and six talents of gold. Beside that he had of the merchantmen, and of the traffick of the spice merchants, and of all the kings of Arabia, and of the governors of the country."

Solomon is the fabulously rich King Solomon, of course, and 666 talents of gold would be 34 tonnes - worth more than four hundred million dollars at today's price.

The Hijaz country of western Saudi Arabia is scattered with the remains of ancient mines; one of them, known as Mahd al Dhahab - or Cradle of Gold - between Mecca and Medina, is now operating again. In its first full year it produced nearly three tonnes. Mining archaeologists reckon it is a reasonable supposition that Mahd al Dhahab was one of the mines from which King Solomon got his gold. The metal has always exerted a special fascination, and two decrees issued earlier this year made it clear that gold would be treated differently from all other minerals in future mining concessions.

99

Foreign companies will not be given exploration rights and will be offered only contract mining - that is, with no share of the gold extracted. There are unconfirmed reports that the Saudis, when sending the gold abroad to be smelted and refined, are making the unusual demand that they want their own gold back, unmixed with anyone else's, and not just payment based on its market value.

Some of the gold will no doubt go to adorn the holy places of Islam in Mecca and Medina. Vast development projects are going on in both cities to enlarge the mosques and modernise all that surrounds them; traditional houses have been obliterated. Parking for tens of thousands of vehicles will be provided by blasting into the mountains - a project, one geologist remarked, that makes your average mine look like a wheelbarrow and shovel job. To give an idea of the scale, a businessman told me that the contracts awarded to the Saudi company involved in the holy places were worth more than the Channel Tunnel.

The Saudi economy is picking up again after the recession of the eighties, and plans are going ahead for a big expansion of oil production capacity and the petrochemical industry. But the biggest growth is likely to be in the private sector and in manufacturing - only just getting off the ground. Despite the difficulties of living and working in Saudi Arabia, it has its attractions for foreign businessmen. The market here isn't formed yet, one said, you can influence it, create demand. It is a rapidly expanding market: the population, though small, is increasing by three and a half or four per cent a year. It is estimated that very soon half the number of people will be under fifteen, and young Saudis have money; that opens up opportunities for selling a whole range of goods, from trainers to cassette recorders, from eye shadow to sand buggies. Consumer sales last year were the best ever. Jeddah is overflowing with shopping centres, with all the famous international names, and the shops are carrying enormous stocks to demonstrate their faith in a dynamic future.

But with the opportunities come two problems; they may seem mutually exclusive but they exist side by side. How to find enough jobs for all the young Saudis to do, and how to fill the jobs in the country's burgeoning industries with properly motivated Saudis so that the large numbers of foreigners can gradually be replaced. It's a question of attitudes; most of those now at an age to start careers have not been brought up with the underlying assumption that they would one day have to work for a living. And many jobs are not socially acceptable - the minimum requirement tends to be a desk of some kind. The situation is changing - some of those working underground in helmets at Mahd al Dhabab are Saudis - but there's a long way to go.

In some ways young Saudis are highly qualified for the modern world: as one observer put it, this is going to be one of the most computer-literate societies in the world. He noted that the Saudi Gazette newspaper often devoted a quarter of its pages to computer matters. So while the authorities devote much thought to keeping out corrupting foreign influences threatening them through satellite television, the changes already underway inside the country seem bound to have a dramatic social impact.

Can the status of Saudi women, whose faces you scarcely see on the streets of Jeddah, remain the same when they will make up more than half of those graduating from university? The ubiquitous veils tend to set them apart. But one image reminded me that they are, after all, not so different from women the world over, and it stays with me now: a woman playing on the swings with her children at sunset by the Red Sea, her long black cloak flying in the wind.

Despite the Soviet withdrawal, the war in Afghanistan between the Mujahedin guerillas and the government of President Najibullah in Kabul has continued. In the Afghan countryside, although people from all sides yearn for peace, the situation has become increasingly prone to lawlessness.

MILKY BOY AND THE ONE-ARMED BANDIT

GORDON ADAM   KABUL   20 JUNE 1990

I n April, a massacre took place on the main road between Herat and Torghundi on the Soviet frontier. It is worth telling the story behind this clash as it clearly illustrates the kind of society which Afghanistan has become and the extreme difficulty of bringing peace back to this beautiful, ruined country.

The incident involved two bands of militia, both armed and paid by the Afghan government to keep this important link to the Soviet Union free from mujahedin attack. The origin of the dispute was sheep rustling. One of the militia leaders, Mohammed Jan, is from all accounts a veteran sheep thief. His left arm was shot off after he was caught red-handed in the act several years ago. But undeterred, Moammed Jan continued in his profession. The object of his attention recently has been the fat-tailed sheep of another militia commander, a Turkoman tribesman with the unlikely name of Milky Boy. Again, Mohammed Jan was caught while rustling, but this time one of his men was killed, and left on the field of battle with his ears cut off.

Now, Mohammed Jan is a Pashtun or Pathan, whose sense of honour was outraged by this act of mutilation. He planned his revenge with care: Milky

Boy's militia had not been paid for several months, and he learned that a convoy carrying the pay-roll would pass close to his village. On the appointed day, Mohammed Jan's men took up their positions in a concrete pillbox conveniently erected by the Russians prior to their departure from Afghanistan last year.

The opening shot from an anti-tank missile destroyed Milky Boy's prized armoured personnel carrier and killed all those inside. Its wreck was still lying on the road when I passed by a few weeks later. The three other vehicles and an estimated Afs 25 million have all disappeared. Mohammed Jan now openly boasts he can afford an expensive foreign-made artificial arm. At least 28 men - some accounts say 40 - were killed in the attack. An indirect victim was Milky Boy himself, who died soon afterwards while being taken to hospital in the Soviet Union, either from heart or kidney failure. His militia headquarters in Torghundi are guarded night and day by two tanks.

As for Mohammed Jan, he is still happily ensconced in his village, behind whose mud walls poke out the muzzles of his quota of tanks, heavy machine guns, mortars and the like. He is now ready to call it quits, but it is highly unlikely that Milky Boy's band will agree. The government hasn't taken any action beyond asking a third militia force - headed rather uniquely for Afghanistan by a woman commander who defected from the mujahedin several years ago - to mediate. The government in Kabul cannot attack Mohammed Jan for fear that he will defect with his impressive display of weaponry to the mujahedin, whose local commander just up the valley is his cousin.

This, in microcosm, is life in Afghanistan today. Some things don't change: my companions from the United Nations and I were treated as honoured guests by all the parties in this little local conflict. Vendettas are nothing new, either, but the awesome fire power which destroys so many lives for so little reason is a product of the war, and the chronic instability which prevents the government - or anyone else - from being able to control law and order. Society has all but disintegrated and tribalism has made a major comeback.

In Afghanistan today there is a whole generation of young men who are uneducated and for whom peace would mean losing the only occupation they know - how to handle a gun. It is a legacy which deeply worries foreign observers working in Kabul, and it is a source of shame to older Afghans who can remember the peaceful times. Walking down a deserted and partially destroyed street in Herat, I was accosted by some children shouting "kharrigi, kharrigi" - foreigner, foreigner - and throwing pebbles. They were chased away by a local shopkeeper who apologised profusely: "They have only known war, they have no education, nothing to do with their lives."

In the cities the civilian population is subjected to daily barrages of cluster rocket fire from the mujahedin, much of it indiscriminate and lethal to non-combatants. Into this chaos, the superpowers continue to pour more rockets and other weapons, both apparently wanting to stop but unable to reach agreement in case the other side benefits. Such fears are largely irrelevant in Afghanistan today: society has disintegrated to such an extent that no-one is likely to be able to take control of the country as a whole for a long time to come. The danger is rather that the continued supply of arms will hasten Afghanistan's slide into complete anarchy, from which a highly unrepresentative but ruthless leader, most probably a hardline Muslim, will eventually emerge on top.

The arms race is also threatening the small positive moves towards reconstruction. The United Nations is doing a remarkable job in the territory controlled by Mohammed Jan and Milky Boy's men in distributing essential wheat supplies without having them stolen by the first warlord whose land the relief convoy crosses. The eastern province of Kunar is enjoying one of its best-ever harvests after being a near desert a year ago, thanks in part to an international effort supplying improved wheat seed and fertilizer. Now the United Nations has been chased out of the area by Arab volunteer so-called fighters, who are fuelling a nasty inter-mujahedin conflict which is likely to be fought out with Saudi-supplied arms on one side and American-supplied weapons on the other.

Cutting off the weapons supplies won't solve Afghanistan's deeply rooted problems but it will be a small crumb of comfort to the many Afghans in the cities, the countryside and the refugee camps who long for peace. And it will serve notice to the extremists on both sides - who alone stand to benefit from the war continuing - that the time for negotiations has come.

In Israel, differences of opinion between secular and orthodox Jews result in a constant public debate over how people should run their lives. From time to time, the political weight wielded by the country's ultra-orthodox rabbis grips the nation's attention. In July, the secular-orthodox divide threw three rather disparate groups together.

THE RABBIS AND THE BELLY-DANCERS

PAUL ADAMS   JERUSALEM   22 JULY 1990

W hat do 20,000 horse-racing fans, ten belly-dancers and a handful of pig-breeders have in common? Not much, perhaps, but in Israel, where the fault lines that exist between religious and secular life periodically result in tremors, sometimes in full-blown earthquakes, all three groups have, in one way or another, incurred the wrath of the rabbis.

The pig-breeders are the most obvious target of the three. The consumption of pork is proscribed under Jewish law, but such is the demand for the forbidden flesh among Israel's more secular-minded citizens, that the breeders are kept busy satisfying the appetite for pork chops and spare ribs.

All this could change if the rabbis - the country's religious arbiters - have their way. Under a law, dubbed, predictably, the pork law, there will be no raising or selling of pigs except in areas with a sizeable non-Jewish population. For the pig-breeders, this means the end of the road. They know it and are confining their struggle to the question of adequate compensation.

For the promoters of a horse-racing extravaganza at Kibbutz Ga'ash, north of Tel Aviv, the battle is just beginning. The meeting, attended by 20,000 eager spectators, was billed as the biggest event of its kind in Israel, but the punters were less than satisfied. There was nowhere to sit, no shelter from the summer sun's harsh glare and, worst of all, no betting. Much of the event consisted, as one disgruntled spectator put it, of "teenagers riding motorcycles, third-rate aerobic dancing groups, a fourth-rate rodeo and a few Bedouins on camels".

Poorly-organised the meeting may have been, but the fact that so many people showed up to watch on that Saturday, horrified religious leaders. An anguished motion was submitted to the country's parliament, the Knesset, by one of the ultra-orthodox parties, condemning this large-scale desecration of the Sabbath.

Prime Minister Yitzhak Shamir, cashing in on the sense of moral outrage, said he felt deeply hurt by the event. His objection, cynics suggested, probably had more to do with proving his religious credentials to the ultra-orthodox ministers who occupy several key cabinet positions.

One of those ministers, incidentally, is Rabbi Raphael Pinhasi, who now holds the communications portfolio. This would be fine, except that the rabbi neither owns, nor watches, television.

Anyway, a Saturday at the races may turn out to have been a costly mistake for Kibbutz Ga'ash. It has already been reported that at least one major medical centre, owned by orthodox entrepreneurs, has cancelled an order of lighting fixtures made at the kibbutz's electrical goods factory. Not only that, but the kibbutz stands to be taken to court for its alleged failure to apply for a work permit under the conditions of the Sabbath Work and Rest Hours Law.

If horse-racing is the subject of orthodox opprobium, no less can be said of belly-dancing, the sensual Middle Eastern dance-form that has taken root in Israel.

Israel's belly-dancers thought they had scored a major victory in May, when Illana Raskin took the orthodox rabbis to the Supreme Court, and won. The rabbis, who have the power to issue kosher food licences, were told that they could no longer blacklist hotels and restaurants where Miss Raskin danced. The rabbis, for their part, argued that it was impossible to supervise food properly with Miss Raskin wiggling her navel at them in what they deemed to be a suggestive manner.

But if the Supreme Court decision represented a blow for belly-dancing, the dispute rumbles on. Ten dancers protested to the chief rabbis of the city of Ashdod, complaining that rabbinical blackmail was still preventing them from performing. It's clear that the rabbis aren't going to take this one lying down.

Pork-breeding, horse-racing and belly-dancing may not represent the most serious issues facing Israel's religious authorities today, but the fact that disputes of this kind continue to take place in Israel demonstrates that the fault lines I referred to earlier are as sensitive as ever.

President Saddam Husein's action in annexing Kuwait has called into question the present shape of the existing Arab world, which. Although he is the leader of a secular, socialist-style state, Saddam Hussein, according to Tim Llewellyn, is calling out in the name of Islam as well as Arab unity, in his campaign for leadership of the Arab world.

HOW LONG, OH LORD, HOW LONG?

TIM LLEWELLYN   NICOSIA   11 AUGUST 1990

One of the paradoxes of post-colonial life is how the once-ruled but now free object to what an Iraqi commentator in August called the spiteful pencil and scissors of the imperialist map-makers. And yet, in the Arab world the leaders cling vigorously to the inviolability of those artificially drawn states.

Kuwait is a country designed by a British administrator called Percy Cox in 1922, although it had started out 240 years earlier as a tiny sheikhdom on a handy patch of shoreline, administered by the Basra vilayet, or district of the Ottoman Empire. On 2nd August Kuwait was swallowed with ease by Iraq. One one of the reasons the Arabs have with unusual, for them, speed fallen into line with the rest of the world in condemning Iraq is because almost all the borders were arbitrarily marked. There are a number of vulnerable little states who can well contemplate, at a menacing neighbour's hands, the same fate as Kuwait's.

One of them, Jordan, is in the most precarious position of all. These past few days have provided a dismal spectacle of the leadership of a once-stable and well-ordered kingdom pulling in all directions at once. King Hussein, a close friend, supporter and ally of President Saddam Hussein, must wonder whether his neighbour also has designs on Jordan. Many disaffected neighbours of Jordan's Palestinian, Bedouin and often fundamentalist Muslim population see Saddam as a hero, a liberator, even, now, a protector of Islam's holiest shrines from the intruding infidels and discredited House of Saud, which opened the gates of Mecca and Medina. He is a man who says what's what and does what has to be done. The support for him from many Jordanians has been made loud and clear in the local press and in street demonstrations and by volunteers for the Iraqi forces in Kuwait. Yet King Hussein also knows that one militarised Iraqi boot too many and too far inside Jordan would give Israel the ideal opportunity to crash into his kingdom and name it the new Palestinian State.

The leaders of the Arab world do not, on the whole, represent the wishes or the feelings of their people. The fear of Saddam Hussein that has finally, with international leadership, galvanised some of the kings and presidents and emirs into action is that of men who thought no brother Arab, however unpleasant, could transgress the unwritten and written laws - destabilise yes, worry and harry yes, abuse and terrorise, oh yes, but not invade, occupy, humiliate and annex. The Arabs of the streets are captivated by this single-minded Iraqi, tired as they are of feeble, aimless and long-perpetuated leadership. The feeling permeates Syria, Egypt, the West Bank and Gaza, and beyond.

If, as many suspect, the American-Arab-international effort to squeeze Saddam Hussein either out of Kuwait or out of power, leaving, presumably, a more acquiescent regime in Baghdad to concur in restoring Kuwait to its former position - if all this is to be a long haul of months rather than weeks, the dangers on the way are enormous, especially for the Arab leaders. The Eastern Arab world, the Gulf and the Levant, has shown itself over its long years of independence and continuing babble about Arab unity to be as sorely divided as ever, with unity meaning, if it could mean anything as it did under Nasser, plans for the hegemony of a particular despot over his neighbours. To fight off the threat of this imposed brand of unity, that most eminent Arab state, Saudi Arabia, has had to ask for foreign protection. The endemic incapability of the present Arab leaderships to protect even their own basic interests has been brutally exposed.

Israel chuckles on the sidelines looking for opportunities, calling out: "We told you so." And yet if it were not for Israel's continued occupation of Palestinian land and its refusal to allow Palestinians their essential rights and homeland, could a man with Saddam Hussein's record evoke so easily this popularity as the potential saviour of the Palestinians, the abadi - the tough guy - of the Arab street?

The dangers of a war spreading beyond the confines of the Gulf must be great the longer the crisis continues. For instance, if economic sanctions do eventually start to weaken Iraqi resolve and Baghdad's volatile leader, seeing his own ability to move forward blocked and his own political future short, does decide to lash out, why shouldn't he lash out at Israel, however suicidal? Where would the Arab leaders stand then? Would they still be backing the American-Saudi crusade for Kuwait if the Arab enemy occupier was at war with Israel?

The economic pressures on the poorer Arab states are going to be enormous. If Iraq and Kuwait are locked off from world commerce for any length of time, the remittances of the Egyptians, Jordanians, Palestinians, Syrians and Lebanese to their homelands will be cut off as well. Tens of thousands of guest-workers will be fleeing home to augment the already bursting ranks of the unemployed and the resentful. Even in the rich Gulf states, the immediate exodus of foreign workers, Europeans, North Americans, Asians, Levantine Arabs, from the foreign-owned and foreign-run companies, head offices, construction sites, banks, travel agents, newspapers, as they close down in fear or from lack of business, is already causing stagnation and lack of confidence.

The future is grim. Saddam Hussein though, however aggressively and destructively, is forcing the Arab world to examine itself more closely than it has done since 1948, when its lack of cohesion helped hand Palestine to the Israelis. A Syrian friend of mine said to me recently: "What we have to decide now is whether Iraq belongs to the Arab world or the Arab world belongs to Iraq." Some are asking a more worrying question: does the Arab world any longer belong to the Arabs?

Westerners are not the only hostages of the Gulf crisis: hundreds and thousands of Arab nationals and Third World migrant workers are desperately seeking a way out of Iraq. The majority head for Jordan, throwing themselves on the mercy of the Hashemite Kingdom.

THE STARVING EXODUS FROM IRAQ

STEPHEN SACKUR   AMMAN   30 AUGUST 1990

There is a very pleasant transport cafe on the main road from Amman to the Red Sea port of Aquaba, where I like to stop for a drink during the long drive south. The owner keeps his establishment spotlessly clean, and he serves up tasty snacks which have won him the loyal custom of dozens of truck drivers. Admittedly, there is a huge poster of a beaming President Saddam Hussein in the cafe window, but in Jordan such images are hard to avoid.

The place is usually filled with the low hum of conversation and the satisfied slurping of soup, but the last time I was there the atmosphere of calm was rudely shattered. Just as I began eating, hundreds of starving Egyptians burst into the cafe. They had arrived by bus and cattle truck from the border post of Ruweished, some 250 miles away. But they had had little to drink and virtually nothing to eat since they left Kuwait some five days earlier.

Before I could say a word, one desperate man had grabbed my bottle of mineral water and swallowed the lot. Another snatched my basket of bread and was immediately surrounded by his starving friends. There was pandemonium all round. The owner and his three waiters were beseiged at

111

the service counter by more than 100 Egyptians desperate for food. Order was restored only when more staff emerged bearing bread and soup in miraculous quantities. The hubbub of Egyptian voices was transformed into relative silence as the refugees concentrated on cramming bread into their bellies as fast as they possibly could.

Such scenes were familiar in Jordan in the days after the exodus of refugees from Iraq and Kuwait began. A country which itself boasts a population of little more than three million couldn't cope with the daily arrival of thousands of penniless refugees, all of whom were hungry and thirsty, most with no idea about how and when they would be able to leave Jordanian territory.

At first officials tried to deny that the problem existed. The refugees flowed in but little was done to establish a coherent, co-ordinated strategy for their shelter and rapid repatriation. Then the authorities in Amman realised that the influx was running out of control, and they panicked. The Interior Minister announced a formal closure of the land border with Iraq, but border officials merely shrugged their shoulders and let the flow continue. It would have been impossible to do otherwise without condeming many refugees to die in the desert.

Further evidence, if any were needed, of the scale of the problem could be found in and around the port of Aqaba, where the backlog of people waiting to catch the ferry to Nuwebeh in Egypt grew daily. 20,000 people were crammed into a transit camp designed to hold 3,000 at most, just outside the town. When I arrived at Aquaba, camp officials were trying to reunite the thousands of travellers with their passports, which had been confiscated at Ruweished. Names were bellowed out though a loudspeaker by a particularly belligerent-looking policeman, and invariably a dozen Egyptians would put up their hands: "That's me! It's mine!" they shouted in unison, usually prompting the policeman to fling the passport in the direction of the nearest man whether his claim was legitimate or not.

Just as Aqaba was rapidly filling up with Egyptian refugees, so Amman became home to tens of thousands of destitute Bangladeshis, Sri Lankans, Filipinos and other Third World nationals. Inside the Pakistani embassy in a rather exclusive part of the city, I found the embassy garden covered in tents and multi-coloured rugs. This was home to 300 people waiting for flights home to Pakistan. Here the mood was philosophical rather than angry. One man told me how he'd had to pawn his watch to pay for the bus ticket from Kuwait City to the Iraqi border. "I left everything behind, everything I'd worked for", he said,"but I escaped with my life so I suppose I can count myself lucky."

In recent days, the numbers coming across the border have been marginally reduced, but no-one believes the flow is about to subside. In private, Jordanian officials talk of at least a quarter of a million people arriving in the next ten days. But now at least the Jordanian relief effort has received international support. The United Nations and the International Red Cross have organised emergency supplies of tents and blankets. medical facilities for the newcomers have been much improved, and refugees are no longer being forced to sit for hours, even days, in the desert.

There is still, however, one big problem. Some of the countries which have thousands of nationals stuck in Jordan - like Bangladesh, for example - are simply too poor to organise special charter flights to get their people home. For these migrant workers, always seemingly at the bottom of the pile, there is nothing to do but wait and hope. As the diplomatic manoeuvering and military planning is played in the Gulf, it is worth remembering that the crisis has already ruined many lives and many thousands of dreams for a better future.

*Following the invasion of his country by Iraq, the Emir of Kuwait and his
government are now living in exile in the western Saudi Arabian resort of
Taif. The British Foreign Secretary, Douglas Hurd, was among those who
called on the Emir in Taif at the beginning of September. Jack Thompson
went with him.*

KUWAITI GOVERNMENT IN EXILE

JACK THOMPSON   TAIF   10 SEPTEMBER 1990

They call Taif a hill resort. It's not immediately apparent when you first
land there. It takes a drive from the airport, set among sand dunes, to
realise that the real Taif is to be found tucked a few miles away among bare
grey mountains of rock and scree rising out of a landscape of desert and
three-lane motorways - for such is modern Saudi Arabia. Up a hill, round a
bend or two, and there sits the Hotel Al Heda, a spanking five-star complex,
now the headquarters of the Kuwaiti government-in-exile.

Ministers and officials in flowing robes, dishdashas and guttras, swish
through the lobby, the conference halls and the coffee shop. Up on the fifth
floor, at least for the time being, for we've been told he moves around from
day to day ever fearful of an Iraqi assassin's bullet, we were received by the
Emir of Kuwait, Sheikh Jaber al Ahmed al Sabah. As he listened politely to
words of encouragement from Mrs Thatcher, conveyed in measured tones by
the Foreign Secretary Douglas Hurd, the Emir looked drawn and downcast.
Would he ever return to a reconstructed Dasman Palace, now shattered by
Iraqi armour? Or would he be condemned to a life of wandering from luxury

hotel to luxury hotel, perpetually going through the motions of government, direction and make-believe control?

His ministers say they're in constant communication with the Kuwaiti resistance movement, harassing Iraqi forces inside the occupied country, picking off Iraqi troops foolhardy enough to wander into the suburbs of Kuwait City. These are the people, we were told, who still manage to run basic services there; water, electricity and emergency clinics. The Iraqis have closed all the hospitals; they've kicked out the patients; and stolen as much as they could of the sophisticated equipment and drugs which Kuwait's oil riches have procured for its health services.

But when we ask Yahya al-Sumait, the articulate Minister of Housing, for details of the resistance - its organisation, its weaponry, its membership - we get the kind of cryptic response Kuwaiti ministers were wont to give visiting journalists in the days when power and money, and not a little arrogance, also brought obfuscation. "We wish to be honest about this", said Mr Sumait, "but because the Iraqis are listening, we must be hesitant. With time you will know more".

Instead, we were regaled with yet another account of the Emir's flight from Kuwait on August 2nd. The Iraqis invaded at 2 in the morning; some members of the government had gathered at the Defence Ministry. When it was realised that the Iraqis' first target was in fact the Dasman Palace, the Prime Minister took to his Mercedes and whisked the Emir and half a dozen members of his immediate family south, towards the border with Saudi Arabia. Other ministers then began to plan their own escape. Mr Sumait said he hid in a beach house until he judged it safe to follow the same route as the Emir. What neither he nor the rest of the cabinet seems to have contemplated was the defence of the country.

With the benefit of hindsight, Mr Sumait and his colleagues have become less hesitant, especially about what they want from Britain and the United States. "U.N. resolutions are hardly worth the paper they're written on," he said, "and any resolution not backed up by force will fail. God knows what games Saddam Hussein will play before sanctions bite." It's fighting talk, but Mr Sumait is not doing the fighting.

At a suggestion that those Kuwaitis brave enough to have stayed behind to continue the armed struggle against the Iraqis might eventually turn away from the Emir and the government in Taif, Mr Sumait mustered all the indignation he could command. "I deny that kind of insinuation," he said, "it's typical of Iraqi propaganda designed to separate the people from their government." And indeed, he and the others are now more concerned to catch up in the public relations stakes in which Saddam Hussein is judged to be well ahead.

So, as a stream of television crews, radio reporters and writing journalists turn up at the Al Heda Hotel, they're also greeted by Mr Lew Allison of Citizens for a Free Kuwait, an American-based organisation run by Mr Allison's real employer, a smart New York firm of public relations consultants and undoubtedly paid for by the Emir. Mr Allison offers editing suites and reams of paper. But he seems superfluous to requirements. The Kuwaiti ministers are making themselves so readily available; after all, they have precious little else to do.

The Iraqi capital, Baghdad, has been the focal point of the crisis in the Middle East. Roger Hearing spent a week there and found the city stubbornly calm, despite threats from the outside world and nationalistic exhortations from Iraq's President Saddam Hussein.

LIFE IN BAGHDAD

ROGER HEARING   BAGHDAD   11 SEPTEMBER 1990

As the dark clouds gather over Iraq and the Gulf, Baghdad, as befits the eye of a storm, remains eerily calm. There are, of course, clearly visible preparations for war - from the ancient ack-ack guns mounted on triumphal arches to the removal of precious artefacts from the city's museums. But an air of calm resignation, or perhaps a belief that the worst won't happen, seems to have overtaken the people.

It is a sleepy city anyway; flat and rather undistinguished, apart from the notoriously overblown monuments to presidential glory: the giant hands with crossed scimitars and the huge Stalinesque statues. It should be said that any attempt to gauge what a Baghdadi really thinks is futile - they've been schooled for too long in the consequences of speaking their minds. No-one I spoke in the market or the mosque was prepared to do other than praise their president and his actions. As a western journalist I might be expected to explain this away by the presence of the gentleman from the Ministry of Information who never left my side, and a claim that underneath it all the people yearned for freedom from a cruel oppressor and were firm Bush and Thatcher supporters. But I don't believe that either.

The few opportunities of speaking to Baghdadis alone - snatched conversations in lifts and taxis; occasional unguarded comments from hotel staff - present a rather different picture. On the two main issues - peace and Kuwait - they do go along with their president and want both. Peace is important to citizens here, who suffered greatly during the country's eight-

117

year war with Iran. Just beside the hotel I was shown what looked like a building site - it was in fact the remains of two city blocks flattened by an Iranian missile in the war of the cities, when each side bombarded the other's capitals. The signs pointing to underground shelters are going up in the city streets again and the citizens must be shuddering at the prospect of another war. On the question of Kuwait, no-one had any doubts it was, and had been, part of Iraq. But why an invasion? Why, they said, an outright military assault when a coup d'etat could have been staged and there would have been tut-tutting, but nothing very much done by the world. In other words, it's not so much Saddam's aims that are in question, but his methods.

What of the man himself? He is ubiquitous. On the road from the airport a sign says: "Welcome to Baghdad - Capital of Arab Saddam". On every wall, at every street corner there are pictures of him. Hours of television time are taken up with his deeds and appearances. Little girls in national dress and veteran soldiers sing songs about him. Criticism would of course be suicidal, but in little ways I believe the big city Baghdadis do have some fun at the expense of the provincial from the little town of Takrit. The pictures of him for instance do sometimes mock in a subtle way. The giant canvas opposite the main hotels shows him in a typically Brezhnev pose, with fur hat, black coat and the dismissive wave that used to come from the Kremlin podium. Another in the Ministry of Information of all places shows him in cool beach gear and dark glasses, incongruously resembling a shot from a fashion magazine.

Perhaps the irony is imagined, but when you look for it, there is plenty of irony in Baghdad. "It's more than just a hotel" says the new poster advertising the Rashid in the north of the city. Indeed it is more than a hotel. Over the last month it's become a detention centre for western men, and latterly women and children displaced from Kuwait. The use of such hostages, considered outrageous in the West, leaves the citizens of Baghdad unmoved. From what I could gather, hostage-taking is considered the traditional weapon in keeping the peace. It's even more legitimate in their view when the forces ranged against Iraq are so great and so powerful. This 'us and them' feeling is beginning to surface, even though there isn't yet any question of outright hostility to westerners. It's more a 'my country right or wrong' attitude. What would clearly be a mistake is to imagine that the fiery words of Saddam Hussein, the calls for the Jihad - the Holy War - and the suggestion that captured American pilots would be eaten are in any way taken to heart by the people of Baghdad. They are relaxed and wily, cunning, and not easily impressed. Despots and invaders have come and gone; Baghdadis will continue to drive their taxis and sell cigarettes at outrageous prices. My driver's final words to me as I left him at the airport were to come back soon for a holiday and tell all my friends to come and use his cab as well. War and crisis, in other words, shouldn't get in the way of good business.

Egypt has taken the leading role in the Arab world in opposing President Saddam Hussein's invasion of Kuwait. In doing so Egypt was accused by Iraq of serving American interests. From Cairo, Barnaby Mason considered how far President Mubarak's strong line against Iraq was supported by ordinary Egyptians.

EGYPT AND THE GULF CRISIS

BARNABY MASON   CAIRO   20 SEPTEMBER   1990

E gyptians like to make jokes about things, and their attitude towards Kuwait is not straightforward. "The Kuwaitis were the nouveaux riches of the Middle East," one friend of mine said, "now they're the nouveaux pauvres." A mock newspaper advertisement announced that a Sri Lankan family was looking for a Kuwaiti maid, putting the boot on the other foot with a vengeance. Taking a different line, another Egyptian commented that even if the Kuwaitis lost their country they weren't so badly off, with their huge investments abroad.

But even if the Egyptians take a somewhat ambivalent attitude towards the Kuwaitis, they certainly don't like the ruthless and bullying behaviour of the Iraqi regime. Commenting on Iraq's historical claim to Kuwait, President Mubarak said that Egypt had historical rights to many places but had never thought of adopting what he called this uncivilised method. He scornfully rejected Iraqi allegations that Egypt was betraying the Arab cause, expressing astonishment that such accusations were levelled by those who had invaded a sisterly Arab neighbour, killed its people and made the survivors homeless.

Mr Mubarak has pursued a confident and uncompromising line against Iraq since the invasion - a marked contrast to his ultra-cautious and sometimes hesitant approach to Egypt's chronic economic problems. One reason for that is his deep anger at being personally deceived, as he sees it, by President Saddam Hussein. In private conversations, he is reported to have given vivid accounts of the assurances he was given in Baghdad only a few days before the invasion: that the Iraqis were only trying to scare the Kuwaitis, that there were no troops near the border. President Mubarak also says the Iraqis tried to buy him off - there's one account of a message relayed through the leader of Yemen offering twenty-thousand-million dollars towards Egypt's huge foreign debt.

The president's strong line is reinforced by overwhelming support from the Egyptian people. There was already great resentment against Iraq: at the end of 1989 large numbers of Egyptian workers there came home complaining of brutal treatment at the hands of Iraqi soldiers returning from the Gulf War. Cairo press reports said Egyptians had been deprived of their savings, beaten and even killed. Now, since the start of the Gulf crisis, nearly three hundred thousand more workers have returned from Iraq and Kuwait. Egyptian television has carried nightly interviews with people complaining that they've been stripped of their belongings by Iraqi border guards; even children's toys have been taken. The criticism has extended to the Jordanians: an engineer who escaped from Kuwait commented bitterly - "What kind of Arab unity can there be when the Iraqis mistreat us and the Jordanians take advantage of our misfortune to sell us a bottle of water in exchange for a watch or a pair of gold earrings?"

There is a ground swell of indignation about all this, and almost everyone knows somebody who has been in Iraq. There is, of course, some uneasiness about the crisis, and suspicion of the role of the United States. One educated, westernised Egyptian believes the whole thing is an American plot to gain permanent military bases in the Gulf; "That's why they didn't prevent the invasion of Kuwait," he said, "even though they knew about it beforehand." Another advocate of conspiracy theory said events had been carefully orchestrated by the West to benefit Israel.

Criticism of President Mubarak's policy has been negligible, even from the opposition parties; though some of their leaders complained that they had been prevented from travelling abroad to attend a meeting of Islamic groups in an attempt to mediate with Iraq. In its early stages, the crisis caused a split within the Islamic trend that generally represents the most substantial opposition to the government. One Islamic paper published contradictory articles within the same issue, reflecting the difficulties of the Muslim brothers and their allies. On the one hand they could not condemn the Saudi authorities, who have given them substantial financial support; on the other, they were horrified at the presence of American and other non-Muslim forces in a land which shelters the most sacred places of Islam.

More recently the arguments have become subtler and more qualified. A well-known preacher, Sheikh Sharaawi, said on television that whereas American forces were in Saudi Arabia in order to maintain oil supplies, the Egyptians were defending the holy places. However, both were in effect protecting the Saudis, so different interests happened to coincide. "They are assisting us," he said, "why should I object?"

Criticism of Iraq, too, has become sharper: Sheikh Sharaawi said the invasion had been dictated by envy - one of the deadly sins; while the Islamic weekly Al Nur - The Light - described Saddam Hussein as standing arrogantly and obstinately against all the world, and thus treading a path that would lead to his doom. Other Egyptian commentators have poured scorn on the Iraqi leader's call for a Holy War: this dictator who claims to be a Muslim, one said, or even a descendant of the Prophet. A pro-government newspaper went still further in vilification, identifying Saddam Hussein with the Ethiopian General Abraha, who in antiquity was reputed to have tried to demolish the Kaaba, the centre of Mecca's most holy shrine. For the moment, support for the Iraqi leader is not a tenable position in Egypt.

AFRICA

November	14	1989	Swapo win Namibian Elections
December	14	1989	Nelson Mandela and President F.W. De Klerk of South Africa hold first talks
February	1	1990	De Klerk lifts 30-year ban on ANC, PAC and SACP
February	11	1990	Nelson Mandela released after 27 years in Prison
September	20	1990	Samuel Doe, President of Liberia, reported killed during a Coup
September	27	1990	Algeria's first President, Ahmed Ben Bella, returns after 9 years of Exile
October	12	1990	Disasters Emergency Committee in London warns of impending mass Famine in Ethiopia and Sudan

*It may be pushing the metaphorically potential omens too far, but the very
parliament in Cape Town that rejected Harold Macmillan's winds of
change speech thirty years ago, was buffeted by a seventy knot hurricane
in February, as the final words were being spoken in a debate on President
de Klerk's unbanning and reconciliation speech of a week earlier.*

WINDS OF CHANGE?

MIKE WOOLDRIDGE   CAPE TOWN   10 FEBRUARY 1990

Inside the House, the leader of the far-right conservatives, Dr. Treurnicht, was saying for the tenth, or was it the twentieth time, that Mr de Klerk had cheated the white electorate. Mr de Klerk had awoken the tiger in the white man, the crocodile in the black man. The Democratic party was complaining that the government had not abandoned race groups as the building blocks of the party constitution. Mr de Klerk was accusing the Conservatives of hysteria, the Democrats of failing to protect minorities and wanting to put South Africa on the path to majority rule. He'd wanted to remove the stumbling blocks in the way of negotiations on power sharing. As clouds exploded off the top of Table Mountain and the windows of the parliament building rattled, the potential volatility of the next phase in South African politics hit the senses too.

And this is before Nelson Mandela has actually emerged from prison. Forty miles from the centre of Cape Town in his warder's bungalow in the grounds of Victor Verster Prison, he was yesterday deeply immersed in politics as well, discussing tactics in the post-banning era with twenty-two members of the United Democratic Front. They came out with the message that he may well not restrict himself on his release to the role of senior statesman, that seems sometimes to be carved out for him. If the government did not act on all the ANC's conditions for negotiations, the main ones left being the complete lifting of the state of emergency and the release of all political prisoners, then Mr Mandela would join the the continuing defiance campaign, break the law and be fully prepared to end up in jail again. Marches of thirty thousand people are not uncommon these days. It doesn't require a great deal of imagination to predict a Mandela-led march several times that size.

The government believes it has regained the political initiative with Mr de Klerk's opening of parliament speech. It knows there is a risk of a serious white backlash. Ministers concede that the Conservatives are likely to win their hoped-for one million recruits among apprehensive whites, and could win an election held today. The argument that the government is trying to put across is that the alternative to what it has done and what it is hoping to achieve through negotiations, is war, and that the government is only having to make a political shift, whereas the ANC is having to abandon any notion of a one party state, and will have to modify its enthusiasm for nationalism. The search for negotiations will not be at all easy, even with Mr Mandela's release, and even if the government does widen its amnesty for political prisoners and scrap the rest of the state of emergency. The government eventually wants to control the negotiating process, offering seats at the table and an open agenda to any leaders and groups committed to peace, the results and constitutional changes probably being put to the existing electorate in a referendum.

T he ANC wants to agree on a mutual cessation of hostilities first, then have non-racial elections to choose the representatives for a constituent assembly on Namibian lines, which would actually draw up a new constitution. But the ANC are anxious not to negotiate in a vacuum. Its early rash of demonstrations under the ANC banner against local grievances, such as poor housing and schooling, has been important in keeping up the pressure on the government and keeping its negotiators in touch with grass roots opinion. There will, of course, be a middle ground in the negotiations as well, represented by people like Chief Buthelezi and other homeland leaders and organisations, and the parties that will have participated in the tri-cameral parliament. From these sources, there are already murmurings about eventual alliances with the ANC, and because of their past association with Pretoria, that is something that will promote vigorous debates within the ANC.

One of Mr Mandela's closest friends, the lawyer and UDF leader Dullah Omar said he tends to underplay the role that awaits him on his release. Even though many say he has exceptional qualities of leadership and determination, it could be that another Mahatma Gandhi is about to appear on the world stage, a figure who continues to facilitate in various ways while the younger generation of ANC leaders concentrate on the transition from liberation movement to a broad-based political party. So it is hardly surprising that, with Nelson Mandela expected to go free at any moment, the weather forecast for the Cape region is continuing gale force winds.

If the South African government really intends to dismantle apartheid, the process will be a unique one. There is great momentum for change, and the country is braced for an exhilerating, if painful, transition.

NEW-STYLE APARTHEID

NIGEL WRENCH   JOHANNESBURG   13 FEBRUARY 1990

P aul Joemat had a furrow in his brow when he hurried out of the back door of the Cape Town City Hall on Sunday evening. Sweat soaked through his khaki shirt with its black, green and gold ANC shoulder flashes. Paul Joemat works as a teacher in a Cape Town township, but is also a political activist of long standing. On Sunday, he was trying to sort out the chaos that Nelson Mandela's welcome home rally had turned into. A political rally where the people, angry and impatient because Nelson Mandela was late -rather than the police - were the main problem.

For once in South Africa, there were no rules for Paul Joemat to follow. Not the rules of old-style apartheid, under which a rally would have been banned, nor of old-style political defiance which would have had Paul Joemat and his colleagues doing their best to break the law. Mr Joemat got through the day, but it wasn't easy. It's not just that the rules have changed; it's an entirely different game. No-one knows what is going to happen next. But one wealthy businessman that I know believes he does know what is going to happen. He was as relaxed as Paul Joemat was tense. This man believes he is going to make a lot of money out of it. "The reasoning is this," he said, smiling over a cup of coffee. "South African manufacturing has found some new markets for its goods to circumvent the effects of sanctions. So," said my friend, "say it's now operating at eight-tenths that it was before sanctions. Add to that the new sanctions trade and you potentially have an economy that grows at seven per cent a year, helped by increased productivity, because the reasoning goes, people now feel they have a stake in the economy."

Business people like my friend are grinning widely. Their investments made, they wait to reap the benefits. Not all whites are worried about these changes. They are economically sound. It is a lot more secure, somehow, than the black, green and gold shoulder flashes and the slogans of the teacher, Paul Joemat. But there are whites who are far more worried and tense, of course. Take Jan Du Toit, who has a small suburban house in the suburb of the city of East London. He, like Paul Joemat, likes to dress in khaki, but their politics could not be more different. For Jan Du Toit is one of the local organisers of the far right wing A.W.B. (Afrikaanse Weerstandsbeweging), the Afrikaner resistance movement known as the AWB. Jan Du Toit doesn't see a post-apartheid society as an opportunity, he certainly doesn't see it as a time for celebration. To him it is simply a threat to the way of life which has allowed him and other whites to use East London's beaches, while the only blacks allowed near the sand were nannies and servants.

That has changed already, and Mr Du Toit is simply waiting now for his first black neighbour. In this household, the name "Mandela" is a swear word. Jan Du Toit says things like, "I don't know what blacks mean when they talk about inequality. They're different from us... They shout across the street to greet each other."

Mrs Du Toit comes out of the kitchen to nod agreement. These protests, she says, are simply the work of "black rubbish." The Du Toits are not waiting to find out if their gardener turns out to be a "black rubbish." They plan to move to a quiet country town where the blacks are more servile and the whites still firmly in control.

Jan Du Toit does not, on principle, buy the Daily Despatch newspaper. This is the paper that Donald Woods, now in exile in London edited - the paper that allowed a voice to Steve Biko, the charismatic activist from this region who died in detention. These days, the Daily Despatch does not carry a column by political activists any more. "Time change", says Glyn Williams, the current editor, who met Donald Woods when they both worked on the Western Mail in Cardiff. Mr Williams' most talked about column in the Daily Despatch these days is called *Farming on Friday.*

But all that may change. Last week, Glyn Williams published the first article by Donald Woods that has been allowed in South Africa since 1977, although you get the sense that it was more by obligation than by deep-rooted political belief. Glyn Williams is certainly a liberal, but perhaps he is one of those whites who sees change as necessary, rather than to belong to those who strive for it. He doesn't frown, celebrate, anticipate business, or condemn. For the time being, the enjoyable life of middle-class whites like Glyn Williams is unlikely to change. Jan Du Toit, with less money to buy privilege, will feel it first. My millionaire friend will not feel it at all. Paul Joemat is feeling it already. He is excited, but exhausted. Maybe that is what change is all about.

*The threatened assault on the Sudan's southern capital, Juba, by rebels of
the SPLA in February was only one sign of the country's deepening crisis.
The military regime that seized power in June 1989 from a democratic,
but largely discredited government, had so far shown little sign of coming
to grips with the situation.*

SUDAN OLD
AND NEW

BARNABY MASON   KHARTOUM   15 FEBRUARY 1990

I t is not too appallingly hot in Khartoum at this time of year and the
bougainvillea makes a spectacular display of red, pink, purple and
orange. The Revolution Command Council, led by General Omar Hassan Al-
Bashir, has spent a good deal of energy smartening up the town, or at least
the roundabouts. One is now full of flowers; another is crowned by a
splayed-leg concrete structure resembling an alien plant, its branches bearing
globes of green and gold like monstrous fruit. The roundabouts look like a
Sudanese version of the creations you see in Saudi Arabia and the Gulf states.

Outside the Council of Ministers an avenue of big old trees has been
savagely pruned; the horticultural equivalent of a military short-back-and-
sides. The potholes in the roads haven't been filled in, as several Sudanese
pointed out; there is hardly any sugar or cooking oil to be had, and black
market petrol costs ten times the official price. But you can't have everything.

A new decree says that all shops must have green doors or shutters with
white surrounds, and the new paint has certainly had an impact on the centre
of Khartoum and Omdurman. The choice of Islamic green was taken as a
sign of the influence of Muslim fundamentalists in the government, though
when I put the point to the Information Minister, he replied innocently that it
was the first time he'd heard that green was the colour of Islam. All things are

possible in the Sudan I suppose; someone else told me that some influential merchant had simply had a job-lot of paint, shade number 66, that he couldn't get rid of.

The Military Council seems to have the lid screwed down pretty tightly on Khartoum. It has cowed many of its opponents into submission, as can be heard in the many stories circulating in town about trade unionists, professional people and academics being beaten and tortured. The government seems determined to prevent a repetition of the mass street demonstrations which brought down a previous dictator, Jaafar Nimeiry, in 1985.

But opposition is still there beneath the surface. Efforts to impose new puppet leaderships on the unions have not worked, and underground newspapers are circulating. I saw one six-page pamphlet put out by the barred Socialist Party; the main article headlined: "The People Are Stronger Than The Tyrant." The paper repeated the charge - officially denied - that the government is effectively run by the National Islamic Front. It recommended a rhythmic chant of defiance for people to use in street protests, and gave detailed figures for the large sums of money allegedly used by the Military Council in travelling abroad.

Apart from more or less keeping control of the capital, it often seems that a Sudanese government is entirely powerless. The war continues to go the rebels' way and the economy is in a worse state than ever. Partly in a spirit of escapism, I went to look round the National Museum before embarking on an archaeological trip down the River Nile.

For about 75 years, I learned, the Sudan was a world power - that was in the eighth century BC, when a king from the ancient realm of Napata in the north conquered Egypt and made himself Pharaoh, founding the 25th Dynasty. The Kingdom of Napata itself, later shifted a little south to Meroe, lasted another thousand years. The museum is full of the artefacts of that civilisation: fine polished pottery, elegant bronze mirrors, beautiful beads and a statue of King Taharqa as an Egyptian Pharaoh with clearly African features.

Together with Sudanese and British archaeologists I travelled north down the Nile, marvelling at the remains of a civilisation whose existence I'd barely suspected; temples, pyramids and palaces, some now crumbling into the dust. Many sites are threatened by modern settlements and agriculture, but the local people don't see why the living should give way to the distant dead.

One old lady, complaining about the lack of electricity and land for housing, remarked bitterly, if unreasonably, that the antiquities were spreading everywhere. The Muslim Fundamentalists are also unsympathetic; after all, the ancient civilisation flourished long before the arrival of Islam; and it was an African civilisation, if also influenced by the Mediterranean. The Sudan in Arabic means 'land of the blacks'. If the present-day war was to end with the country being split into two - an Arab north and an African south - it would be a profoundly symbolic break with the past.

Natural disasters happen so often around the world that after a while they seem to merge into one another. But for the people who survived that flood, drought, or earthquake, the effects don't go away: they have to re-build their homes and their lives. In late January, central and southern parts of Tunisia were hit by severe flooding.

TUNISIA AFTER THE FLOODS

PETER HIETT   TUNISIA   27 FEBRUARY 1990

One month after the floods, it was only when we cut inland that the lasting effects started to appear. Driving across the northern flank of the Sahara Desert, from the coastal town of Gabes to our destination of Gafsa, huge holes suddenly appeared in the road, where the angry waters had simply ripped away great chunks of tarmac. In three places, the low bridges which usually carry the road over the dried up river-beds had been destroyed. We made detours over the rutted sand; it was like driving on snow, except that on each side, a brazen sun beat down on the arid plains stretching to a hazy horizon.

There has always been some life here: a few olive trees, some goats - enough to support a sparse population - and water, too: the occasional well, and a couple of shallow lakes permanent enough to be marked on maps. But those yellow and purple shrubs looked too fresh to be able to survive the relentless heat year in, year out. And surely no-one would build a house in the middle of one of those shallow lakes? But there was its roof, with the tops of some olive trees around it, just emerging from the water. Another bend in the road took us to a large body of water that wasn't marked on any map. These were new lakes - perhaps permanent - formed by the floods in a region that is usually surprised and grateful to get any rain at all.

The story of Tunisia's floods is one of disappointed hope. The country was delighted when the rains began. There had been two years of drought: farmers, and the economy as a whole, had suffered. Around the oasis of Gafsa, the drought had lasted four years. But instead of stopping, the rains grew heavier. Dried-up rivers trickled, then roared back into life. Wells overflowed, then collapsed. Bridges, roads and railways were destroyed. And people died. Country-wide, at least thirty: with a population of eight million, it could have been worse. In Gafsa, only one - out of nearly three hundred thousand. But it had cost a lot to put the damage right: about two hundred and fifty million pounds - a great deal for a relatively poor nation like Tunisia.

In the Gafsa region, the governor, Mr Mohammed Ben Rejeb, estimated the final bill at perhaps twenty million pounds. Desert houses are built of mud, to keep cool in hot weather; in floods, they simply melt away: twenty four thousand buildings in the Gafsa region were damaged or destroyed, and the kaleidoscope of figures went on; two thousand wells destroyed, twenty five thousand blankets and eight hundred tents distributed, ten thousand loaves of bread helicoptered around the region in the first twenty four hours of the flooding. The figures were all there, stored in the computerised control room the governor set up when it became clear that big problems were on the way. As he told it, the story unfolded like a military campaign.

A s soon as the weather service told him the rains would continue, he convened a meeting of the regional safety commission. They sent an army detachment to a particularly vulnerable town; later that night, it rescued the passengers from a stranded train. By four in the morning, local centres were virtually cut off from one another. As relief aid started arriving it was logged in - on that computer system - and logged out again. Places that couldn't be reached by road had food ferried out by helicopter. Earth-moving equipment from the local phosphate-mining company was requisitioned to quickly clear the roads of mud. The railway lines that take the phosphate to the ports were repaired. Phase One was over.

Phase Two was still going on. On the individual level, people's homes would have to be rebuilt; money was being distributed to them. We saw a noisy queue outside a municipal office waiting for the grants. Agriculture would have to get going again: teams had been out repairing the vital wells and greenhouses, for fruit-growing. The major construction work had also begun: roads and bridges would have to be repaired - perhaps made stronger this time, so that the next floods wouldn't do so much damage. And flood protection barriers would have to be built around Gafsa town itself and other threatened areas. This was long-term stuff, but the plans were ready, work was due to start soon.

The floods a story of disappointed hope? Well, not here, according to governor Ben Rejeb. He said the benefits would outweigh the disadvantages in Gafsa, where ground-water reserves had been so replenished that local development could be speeded up, where long-since dried-up lakes had reappeared, like the ones we saw, and where the goat-herds could feed their animals on those bright new plants, now that the floods had come to Gafsa, to make the desert bloom.

The ivory trade has caused a drastic fall in the African elephant population, now believed to be less than half the figure ten years ago. International agreement was reached in October 1989 to ban the buying and selling of ivory. Kenya is in the vanguard of the fight to stamp out the trade.

THE TROPHY ROOM AT TSAVO

ALEX KIRBY   NAIROBI   17 MARCH 1990

Travelling around Kenya by light aircraft, as we did, you often see elephants. When we put down on one landing strip our pilot had to pull up fairly promptly because two elephants were wandering slowly across the far end of the strip. But the records tell a different story. Twenty years ago, we heard, Kenya had about one hundred and sixty five thousand elephants. Today it has around sixteen thousand. Ninety per cent have gone. And if the ivory poachers had their way, the rest would follow soon enough.

But it is beginning to look as if the poachers may not have their way. Over the last year the Kenya Wildlife Service has been transformed. It was at one stage at least part of the problem, though no-one will say how much poaching it did itself. It is now well-armed, well-paid, and - to judge from the rangers and wardens we met - highly motivated. The Wildlife Service is on the point of doubling the number of armed men it can send into the bush against the poachers.

Their weapons are not simply for defence. In the national parks and reserves, the patrols are under orders to shoot to kill if they encounter

136

anyone carrying firearms which have not been declared in advance. In ten months between sixty and a hundred poachers have been killed - the exact figure is vague because some of those hit vanish into the bush, to die there unrecorded. In the same period the Wildlife Service has lost two of its own men. That apart, it says several hundred poachers have been arrested, and a similar number have given themselves up. Some are even being trained as rangers.

The government explains this determination to eradicate the poachers by saying that the elephants - and all of Kenya's wildlife - are a national resource. They are what tourists come to Kenya to see. And tourists bring in more foreign currency than anything else. The poachers, of course, are not the only threat to the elephants, though they are certainly the most urgent. Because it is sometimes hard to persuade people that allowing elephants to survive, rather than killing them when they wander onto your crops, is a patriotic duty, the government is exploring ways of helping local communities to derive some direct economic gain from tolerating wild animals.

I had expected that many Kenyans would be entirely hard-headed about their animals. I was wrong. One senior warden in Tsavo National Park, which has suffered badly from the poachers, told me he was sometimes reduced to tears when he came across their victims.

It certainly seems true that elephants evoke a curious sense of affinity in many people. Perhaps it is the similarities between their development and ours. They remain physically dependent on their mothers till they're about six years old. They pass through puberty at about fifteen. And - given a chance - they'll live to about seventy. And not only do they remember - they also learn. We heard more than once how the elephants had learnt not to loiter in places where they might be shot, but would pass through as quickly as possible, not stopping even to eat. In Tsavo, where I was told that elephants had learnt that the price of survival is avoiding human contact, I was struck that one herd let us get to within fifty yards of them. The explanation was simple. We were near the rangers' headquarters, and the elephants had learnt that here was an oasis of safety in an otherwise hostile landscape.

It was in Tsavo that I was brought up short against one aspect of the ivory trade that seemed to me to epitomise why it is simply wrong. At the park headquarters the rangers have a trophy room. It contains an assortment of captured weapons - bows, arrows, a home-made muzzle-loader. There are wire snares and steel leg-hold traps, and a pile of lion and cheetah skins. And there are tusks - almost all of them from animals killed after last October's international agreement to stop trading ivory, and suggesting that the market is still very much alive. Some of the tusks are from elephants of perhaps forty or fifty years. And some, the smallest, stand out white and clean, too young yet to have been stained and pitted with the red earth of Tsavo. They come from animals three or four years old when they were killed. It is a charnel house.

There is a determination that the trophy room will not fill up again. The rangers know the risks they run, but once on the poachers' trail they don't give up. Another trail is leading to Kenya's influential ivory dealers - people in business, politics, even government. The head of the Service, Dr Richard Leakey -who has a bodyguard - thinks he and his men are winning. "The ivory trade", he told us, "is going the way of the fur coat - and fast".

In March, Africa's most important football tournament - the African Nations Cup - took place in Algiers. The finals, involving eight nations, are played over a fortnight. In 1990 the host country, Algeria, beat Nigeria 1-0 in the final to win the cup for the first time.

A GREAT DAY FOR ALGERIAN FOOTBALL

JONATHAN BIRCHALL   ALGIERS   18 MARCH 1990

A lgiers is a city where the process of decay outstrips that of renewal. Sitting piled up on a promontory overlooking the Mediterranean, the white stucco facades of the old French buildings crumble, the paint peels. In the Place de la Grande Poste, a sign announces a delay of at least thirty months on a building site where no-one seems to be working.

But while the city's material structure decays, its population grows. More than fifty per cent of Algerians are under eighteen. Algiers is a city of young people, of young men and boys who stand in groups on the cracked and broken staircases which run up from the centre of town. It is also a city of football: three games at once on a small six-a-side pitch near the university, complete with balls, shirts and floodlights. Or played with a stone by a group of small boys in amongst the pedestrians by a monument to an Algerian national hero. Or even with a stuffed plastic bag, on an impossibly sloping pavement.

They play football, said one of my taxi drivers, because there's nothing else to do. As in many other countries, football is a distraction from the frustrations of poverty and unemployment - the same frustrations which just over a year ago led to major anti-government riots in the city, which were put down with heavy loss of life by the army. Since then, the ruling party has instituted political reforms, and Algeria is on its way to a multi-party system.

But the anger remains - when the President, Chadli Ben-jedid, appeared at the stadium for the final of the African Nations Cup, sections of the crowd broke off from their enthusiastic singing of the national anthem, chanting instead: "Jayish, Shaab, Abbas Medeni, Jayish Shaab Abbas Medeni" - the army, the people, and the name of the leader of Algeria's most radical Islamic opposition party.

Two hours before the kick-off, the stadium was already full - 80,000 singing and chanting fans, waving green, red and white flags, some in headbands, and face paint, others waving vast models of the cup they were sure their team was going to win. Outside the stadium there were riot-police and watercannon, inside, police with helmets and shields ringed the pitch.

For half an hour, the Nigerians held the crowd in suspense, the tension edging towards frustration as the Algerians failed to make any headway against a team they beat 5-1 at the beginning of the tournament. Then, in the 38th minute Oudjani made himself an Algerian national hero, shooting past the Nigerian keeper. The stadium virtually exploded - there were rockets shooting into the air, orange smoke bombs, and distress flares, flying high above a mass of green and white Algerian flags. The military band there for the national anthems began a programme of extempore music making, which continued right up to the final whistle.

After the triumph of the national team, the fans began their own triumphal march on the city - a vast column marching on foot back towards the city centre, decked in palm branches, chanting and shouting, chanting "One, two, three, Vive Algerie", and "Jaysh Shaab Abbas Medeni". The city centre they made their own - cars hurtling through the streets, horns blaring with flags and fans hanging from the windows.

It was the biggest party for the city's football fans since Algeria beat West Germany in the World Cup in 1982 - an event now firmly inscribed in the national consciousness. And the triumph was in its way a brief popular uprising, the normally strict rule of law suspended, in a mood of fevered excitement, stopping just short of violence. A great day for Algerian football.

But the wild celebrations are rooted ultimately in political discontent - and in problems that won't be solved as easily as winning the African Nations Cup.

Ivory Coast has a reputation as an oasis of calm and stability in West Africa, but it was plunged into political crisis. The trouble started when students in the capital, Abidjan, went on strike in protest at a decline in living standards that has left many of them unable to pay their rents. Since then, there have been a series of violent demonstrations against an austerity programme which is going to mean big pay cuts for public and private sector workers.

THE BASILICA IN THE BUSH

ADAM CURTIS   ABIDJAN   20 MARCH

W ithin a few hours of arriving in the country, I found myself in Abidjan's ultra-modern Cathedral, watching about two hundred students trying to hold a meeting. No hard-line militants these; just a bunch of very nervous kids sounding off in excited whispers about what they see as increasing political repression by the government of President Houphouet-Boigny. A priest was pleading with them, persuading them that this was not the place to be holding a meeting of this kind and eventually leading them in prayers.

But while all this was going on, the police and military presence outside was growing. The situation began to generate its own tension; the students inside afraid to leave, the police outside apparently uncertain how to react. Their almost complete inexperience in dealing with political dissent is perhaps the nearest they have to an excuse for what was to follow.

For a couple of hours, there was a stalemate. Several hundred more students gathered across the road from the Cathedral. Members of the clergy were trying to mediate. Then, as darkness began to fall, the riot police moved in. A large dark van drew up in front of the crowd; blue-helmeted men leapt from the back. The students took flight, stampeding in all directions away from the van. But the police were already on top of them, lashing out ferociously with their rubber truncheons and dragging at least a dozen away.

Later - in the early hours of the morning - the students still inside the Cathedral were persuaded to leave with a promise from the police of safe conduct back to their lodgings. The priest who had earlier led them in prayer agreed to go with them. It seems that, once inside the police vans, they were roundly beaten up and taken into detention. The priest too was hit around the face and body, his robes torn.

This incident - which led to a significant increase in the level of unrest - is completely untypical of life in Abidjan - normally a calm, cosmopolitan city. But the following day, I caught a bus up to the federal capital, Yamoussoukro - also the birthplace of President Houphouet - and there, it is easy to get some sense of what lies behind the political unrest. A bizarre transformation has been brought about in this ordinary little African town. Deserted eight-line highways gouge their way through its centre and there is a collection of some of the most stunning pieces of modern architecture I've ever seen: the Houphouet Foundation with a two-and-a-half-thousand seat conference hall that would make a comfortable home for the United Nations General Assembly; two colleges of Higher Education set in exotic landscaped grounds; a luxury hotel with manicured golf course and the President's own residence with its crocodile-infested moat.

Most extraordinary of all perhaps is the notorious Basilica modelled on St Peter's in Rome, its great dome rising eerily above an African landscape of tin-roofed homes and chaotic cultivation. President Houphouet is said to be greatly put out at the apparent reluctance of the Pope to return to Ivory Coast to consecrate the country's second great Cathedral. Among ordinary Ivorians, there seems to be a growing sense of injustice that such extravagance should exist in their midst while they continue to suffer the consequences of the downward trend in the prices of coffee and cocoa - the country's two main exports.

Cynics among them say the aged President is trying to buy his way to heaven. And there are those who, after the events of recent days, are predicting that the price of that ticket to eternity may well have gone up.

143

Changes could be on the way, for Algeria with the passing of a Landmark Act which is meant to restructure the country's economic landscape. The country's parliament voted it into law just a few hours before the beginning of the Moslem holy month of Ramadan, when Moslems fast during daylight hours.

ALGERIA DURING RAMADAN

PETER HIETT   ALGIERS   8 APRIL 1990

Life in Algiers turns upside down during Ramadan. During the day, the streets are virtually empty; telephones are frequently left to ring; and if they are answered, the man you want to talk to - and in Algeria it nearly always is a man - is usually in a meeting. It's not said, but it is understood, that these meetings generally involve a soft pillow and a darkened room. The man you want is asleep, staving off the pangs of hunger and thirst, and catching up on all the sleep he didn't get the night before.

At night, it's a different world. Shops and food stalls do a roaring trade, even the zoo is open until the early hours of the morning, and families crowd the streets. You never see women outside after dark during the rest of the year; they don't want to run the gauntlet of jeers and sometimes assaults from the knots of unemployed youths who lounge at every corner.

But Ramadan is different; though in some ways, it could be said to be a truer reflection of Algerian life than the rest of the year is. Take, for example, the way life only really gets going after dark, with daylight activity reduced to a minimum. Large parts of the economy work just like that. Do you want to buy a foreign brand of cigarettes? Well, there's no point trying a tobacconist's shop. The small stock it received from the cigarette factory was instantly

144

bought up by a middle-man, who in turn passed it on to a street-vendor, who's now selling the cigarettes at twice the official price. You have to go to the grey market. How about a tyre for your car? As ever, ask a taxi-driver. In fact, he'll probably tell you without you having to ask. It starts on your ride in from the airport. The driver will offer to change money for you, at twice or perhaps three times the official rate. He needs the foreign currency so he or one of his friends can go to France to buy spare tyres: none are available in Algeria, so unofficial imports are the only solution. Incidentally, you shouldn't accept his offer for two reasons. Firstly, it's against the law to change money on the black market, and you could have problems when you leave the country; and secondly, he's cheating you. You can get six times the official rate elsewhere.

These are not isolated examples; construction takes much longer in Algeria than it should because there's a chronic shortage of raw materials. Textile factories have been closing down for the same reason. The state is unable to keep its supermarkets fully stocked, so people buy privately, at high prices - higher still, in Ramadan. And the list goes on ... the economy is full of corrupt practices and shady dealers; but perhaps that's not surprising when its most active parts are precisely in the shadows.

Now, though, after nearly thirty years of state socialism, the government is introducing economic changes as revolutionary as any taking place in Eastern Europe, changes that will affect everyone from the lowest paid factory worker to giant multi-national companies. The most immediate effect for most Algerians is an end to the virtual immunity from the sack they have enjoyed until now. A new labour law permits lay-offs, redundancy and early retirement for companies in economic trouble - a description that applies to the vast majority of Algerian firms. So the new law could put an end to the inefficiency and strike-happiness that has helped bring the country into its current economic difficulties, despite its enormous oil reserves.

Chances for prosperity are being reinforced by another new law, on money and credit. This one lifts many restrictions on foreign investment, and in theory opens the way to wholly foreign-owned companies, finally bringing genuine competition to stimulate the lazy and inefficient state firms into providing a genuine service to their customers. Various technical measures are also being taken involving the role of banks, and more particularly the central bank, with the aim of soaking up all the spare money currently hanging around.

Algeria still has a long way to go to put its economy right and use to the full its undoubted natural and human resources. The social and political problems which finally convinced the country's leaders that they needed to change their economic course will undoubtedly make taking these measures all the harder. But foreign investors are already expressing interest: the country is a viable proposition. It seems that Algeria's long economic night may finally be coming to an end.

Even after talks began in April 1990 to end the civil war between the Angolan government and the UNITA rebel movement, some of the fiercest fighting continued in the south east of the country, around the UNITA stronghold of Mavinga. Most Angolans hoped that Mavinga would prove to be the last such battle in the fifteen year conflict.

A VISIT TO MAVINGA

JULIAN BORGER   MAVINGA, ANGOLA   16 MAY 1990

The last time I went to Mavinga, I flew. On that occasion, in late January, a chartered Dakota plane, about forty years old, went straight from South Africa to the airstrip that gave this ruined town its strategic importance. Since that visit the airstrip has been blown up, apparently by UNITA in order to rob the government of its use if Mavinga fell, and so this, my second journey, was a less comfortable one.

The Dakota this time went only as far as a UNITA base one hundred miles to the south, at a place called Licua. From there, the route ran overland on sand tracks through southern Angola's tinder-dry forests: a journey that took over twenty five hours. As one battered truck broke down, so another would, after an hour or two, emerge out of the forest to take up the journey. On the last leg, a lorry was sent from Mavinga personally by the UNITA leader, Jonas Savimbi, concerned at the non-appearance of sixteen visiting journalists. We, the sixteen, were meanwhile huddled under blankets at the back of the truck, grimly recalling how the trip had been made to sound almost like a jaunt in the country by UNITA's slick Washington-based public relations firm.

Appearances have become all-important in this war, where the struggle to keep arms flowing from the US Congress is as vital as the fighting inside Angola itself. In every hut in every UNITA camp, I saw a framed picture on the wall showing Dr Savimbi sitting alongside former US President Ronald Reagan. As I arrived in the middle of the night at Licua, I was handed a form that demanded to know whether I had a confirmed reservation for my return journey, on what flight, and on what airline. "You can leave that blank", my UNITA minder told me. It was, after all, part of the great fantasy; the fantasy that pictures Licua as a busy airport, at which international travellers would arrive or make onward connections, not just a clandestine runway, where unmarked light planes piloted by anonymous, tight-lipped South Africans touched down only under the cover of darkness.

What matters for UNITA is the question of legitimacy. The MPLA government in Luanda has none in their eyes as it only survives, they argue, because of Cuban support. The government says very much the same thing about US and South African assistance to UNITA. But with Cuban and South African involvement now wound down by international agreement, and the American and Soviet backers of each side fast tiring of fighting proxy wars, many hope that Mavinga will be the last major battle either side will be able to afford. UNITA was, of course, keen to prove it was a battle the rebels had won, and that was the reason journalists like myself were there. Their base at Mavinga certainly seemed to have survived intact, but much of the surrounding countryside showed the signs of a devastating battle.

Some ten kilometres to the north-west the forest gave way to wide expanses of sand. The trees had all been burnt away by a furnace-like heat that had turned the rest of the vegetation to a greyish dust. Littered across this wasteland were the charred remains of expensive military hardware, and here and there, a makeshift cross, to which an old tin had been nailed and filled with oil to form a rudimentary lantern, lit in honour of the soldiers buried below. It struck me that these men had died just as the politicians back in Luanda were beginning to admit that perhaps the one-party system was not the only option for the country and that perhaps elections could be considered after all, an about-turn that must surely pave the way for a peace agreement.

On the jolting ride back from the battlefield, a soldier standing next to me on the truck dropped a grenade. It rolled sickeningly around my feet for a few seconds, before he managed to pick it up and pocket it, laughing out loud. With the war all but over, how ironic it would be to die by mistake.

Civil war in Liberia broke out during the Christmas week of 1989.
After several months of fighting, the rebels were poised to take the capital,
Monrovia. Elizabeth Blunt was forced to leave a city in turmoil.

LIBERIA :
STATE OF SIEGE

ELIZABETH BLUNT   MONROVIA   13 JULY 1990

T he war crept up on Monrovia almost unnoticed. The first sign that the rebels were finally at the gates was the dawning realisation that not just a few people, but the whole city, was without water; suddenly, the streets were full of people with buckets searching for a source of supply. Water board engineers sent to investigate couldn't get through to the reservoir because of fighting in the area. Two days later, without warning, all the lights went out.

It was just six months since the war had started in the West African state of Liberia, far away on the north-east border, with an attack on an isolated customs post by a handful of men armed with shotguns. Liberian exiles did mount such attacks from time to time; no one took much notice. But this time the movement had been taken in hand by Charles Taylor, a rich, if shady businessman with a great deal of ambition and a flair for publicity. While his lads attacked Butuo, he was ringing up the BBC. And the Liberian government over-reacted. Soon a whole battalion was in Nimba County, where the raid took place, with *carte blanche* to beat up the local population. The rebellion had no great ideological base; the rebels wanted a Liberia still doing business, still tightly linked to the United States, but without President Doe, who they classed as ignorant, tribalist and brutal. What the army reprisals did was to turn it into a popular uprising in Nimba

County.

The actual assault on Monrovia began on a Monday morning, one that in retrospect seems like the city's last morning of innocence. At half past seven, the phone rang and a friend in the outlying village of Caldwell told me, against a background of gunfire, that the rebels were there. The turn-off to Caldwell lies just beyond Monrovia's port, so I set off with a colleague in a rented taxi to see what was happening. At the turn-off, we found a crowd of about a hundred, mostly young men and boys. Cheerfully watching the show, some of them perched on piles of planks for a better view. There was distant gunfire, and soldiers were strung out across the Caldwell Road. Every so often, a pick-up truck full of retreating troops would career off towards town.

A s we headed back to the centre of the city, we spotted a shop selling camping stoves and made a note to buy one as soon as we had checked on the military situation with the Ministry of Defence. But the offices of the minister and chief of staff were locked and empty. In the streets outside, frightened soldiers milled about; a colonel asked us what was going on.

In the time it took to discover that no one at the ministry knew anything, every shopkeeper in Monrovia had shut up shop. We arrived home, without the camping stove, to find the international phone lines cut and the radio station off the air. When I rang, the phone was answered by an alarmed announcer, holed up in the studio, who said there were soldiers in the radio compound and he could hear heavy firing from the direction of the transmitter just as it stopped broadcasting.

People kept arriving at our house; a distraught photographer accompanied by an even more distraught taxi driver; the cameras and the car had been taken away from them by soldiers at gunpoint. Then came a Liberian colleague; he had just phoned his house in the eastern suburb of Paynesville and found that it was already behind rebel lines. At that point, it looked as if things would be over very quickly, although for three weeks the rebel lines hardly advanced at all.

For the first week after the rebel attack, there was anarchy in Monrovia. Government offices were empty, all shops and markets were full of soldiers roaming the streets and looking for trouble. Everywhere, there were apparently derelict cars - their owners had taken off the wheels to stop them being stolen. At night, in the blacked-out city, under cover of a six-to-six curfew, the soldiers could do what they liked. While people cowered in their houses, listening to gunfire echo through the darkness, gangs of soldiers shot the locks off warehouses and supermarkets, and carted away the contents.

An elderly restaurant owner watched from his bedroom window as soldiers came back four times in a pick-up truck to take away food, drink, plates, tablecloths, even the chairs from his restaurant, firing into the air as they did so. In the morning, the Ministry of Defence sent someone to collect a gun which one of the raiders had left behind.

People wounded or killed in the firing were left where they fell. Even ambulances were hijacked by the soldiers, and Red Cross workers were threatened and humiliated at gunpoint. The Italian ambassador was found one morning on his terrace, peering distractedly at a bloated corpse on the beach below his house. He himself was in a great state because he couldn't get through to the proper authorities. A more robust colleague pointed out that there were no proper authorities any more; faced with the same problem a few days earlier, he'd found a couple of strong young men with shovels and buried the body himself.

But people can learn to live with anything. By the second week, the morning search for food and water had become almost routine; some shops began to open briefly and the first private cars ventured out on the road. A few civil servants even turned up for work, which was a mixed blessing for the BBC because one of the first acts of the revived Ministry of Information was to withdraw my accreditation and ask me to leave the country.

Leaving Liberia was easier said than done; just a week earlier, it would have been impossible. In the end, my way out was aboard a battered Russian Antonov military transport plane, originally leased, together with Boris, Vladimir and Sacha to fly it, by a company that planned to make money by flying internal flights around Liberia. But the war intervened, and soon they were flying one of the most extravagantly Wild West operations on the West African Coast. Each day, they made a run into Monrovia and spent the day flying people, goods and arms up to President Doe's home town in the north-east. This was strictly business. The company manager's first job when he arrived in Monrovia was to get the president out of bed and collect the day's fee in cash - American dollars. In the afternoon, they would head the plane for Sierra Leone, cramming into the hold anyone who could pay. There were a few old bus seats up the front; the rest had to squeeze on to canvas benches, perch on the baggage or stand. Every day, the risks became greater and the price went up - 100 dollars, 250, 400, 500 ...

On the day I left, they took 30,000 dollars but, as we took off, there were armed soldiers chasing us down the runway, demanding money. The manager was pacifying them with shouted promises out of the half-open cargo door, and yelling at Sacha to keep going.

With well-armed rebels only five miles away from the airfield, the pilot climbed sharply up and out to sea, the engines straining and a long plume of dark exhaust trailing behind. The passengers, unrestrained by seat belts, slid down the benches and piled on top of one another. They were leaving homes, businesses and, in my case, a job only half-done.

Even so, it was sweet to leave Liberia.

In Liberia, news of the death of the country's President Samuel Doe was confirmed in mid-September, bringing another phase in the West African state's bloody civil war to an end.
At the time, Elizabeth Blunt was the only western journalist in the Liberian capital, Monrovia.

THE DEATH OF PRESIDENT DOE

ELIZABETH BLUNT   17 SEPTEMBER 1990

F or months Liberians had talked of little else; if Doe would go and when Doe would go. Everyone had a different scenario: he would finally lose his nerve and beg the Americans to helicopter him out; he would leave Monrovia for his home village and make a last stand among his own people; or perhaps he would stay until he went down in the flames of his bunker, the Executive Mansion. What no-one ever thought to imagine was the way that President Doe did meet his end - being carried off from under the noses of an international peace-keeping force in a hail of bullets.

By the beginning of September, the situation in Liberia had reached one of its periodic states of uneasy equilibrium. Rebel leader Charles Taylor and his men had taken most of the countryside, but not the seat of government, where Doe was still clinging on, or the port area of Monrovia, which was held by a rival rebel faction. Five west African countries had tried to break the stalemate by sending in a joint force with a mandate to negotiate and maintain a ceasefire, and to use it to bring in an interim government which would hold the ring until elections could be held.

The peace-keeping force worked slowly, but two weeks after it landed it had made some modest progress. Those men of the rebels in the port area -

Prince Johnson's faction - had agreed a ceasefire and West African troops had gradually deployed in their areas, despite harassment by Charles Taylor's forces. For what was left of the civilian population of Monrovia, there was now a little space in which they could move fairly safely.

But the city was a sad sight. Past the bullet-holed buildings and the wrecked cars, endless lines of thin, weary people trekked to and fro all day long searching for food. The city was under siege; no ship had come in since July and no produce from the countryside could get into town. Liberians basically live on rice, and rice had finally run out. Now there was nothing except boiled wild greens and whatever could be stolen from the port. One day street vendors might have boiled sweets, another day it would be mayonnaise. The mayonnaise is sold by the tablespoonful; it is a common sight to see customers dipping their fingers in their spoonful and licking, licking, licking just to stay their hunger.

I t was at this point that President Doe, who had not been seen out since July, took it into his head to visit the peace-keeping force in its port headquarters. He swept in with a large entourage; ministers, television cameramen and a heavily-armed guard, and he went up to see the force Commander, General Quainoo. But ten minutes later another line of jeeps burst into the port, this time carrying the rebel commander Prince Johnson and his young fighters, flaunting scarlet T-shirts and curly permed wigs, and armed with every conceivable kind of weapon. Members of the rebel group swear that they didn't come to the port to kill the president. But when he arrived unexpectedly, on what they thought was their territory, the opportunity was too good to miss.

Soon there was a full-scale row going on between the two groups; voices were rising and guns were being cocked. Prince Johnson himself, flamboyant and irascible, was stamping about shouting and raving as officers from the peace-keeping force tried to calm him, fumbling with shaking hands to open him a can of beer. The he went to the window and shouted: "Men! Open fire! Open fire!" and the gun battle began.

At least from inside the force headquarters it certainly sounded like a battle, a battle fought at close quarters with rifles, machine guns, grenades and even anti-aircraft guns. For an hour and a half the only sound apart from the gunfire was the begging and pleading of officers from the peace-keeping force trying to stop the carnage. For, in reality, it was less a battle than a massacre, as the rebels mowed down the president's people, chased them into port buildings and machine-gunned them where they were hiding.

When they finally pulled out the president, shot him in both legs, bundled him into a jeep and drove away, they left 78 bodies behind, all from the president's entourage. They took President Doe to the rebel base-camp. Whatever happened that night can only be imagined: by the following morning the president's body was on public display, its fingers smashed, its ears and private parts missing. It was a bloody end for one of Africa's worst rulers.

In a sense that was the moment that everyone had been waiting for for months. And yet so far it has solved nothing. Now the two rival rebel groups are slugging it out for dominance, with the peace-keeping force getting more and more drawn into the fighting. The day before the shoot-out, a team of six aid workers arrived to assess how they could get food and medicine to people in Monrovia. The day they arrived, the port was being shelled. The next day, it was the scene of Doe's capture. The following two days, stray bullets were flying in the centre of town where the aid workers were staying. They left without having seen more than a couple of square miles of the city, and with the message that until the fighting stops, it is going to be very, very hard to send in any kind of help.

*Since the Spanish colonisers withdrew in 1976, the Western Sahara has
been occupied by and integrated into neighbouring Morocco.
Mark Doyle visited some of the towns in Western Sahara administered by
Morocco, and the desert beyond which is scattered with the camps of
Polisario guerillas.*

THE WESTERN SAHARA FROM BOTH SIDES

MARK DOYLE   LAYOUNNE   14 JULY 1990

The little town of Layounne, the capital of the former Spanish Sahara,
echoes to the sound of Moroccan concrete mixers and Moroccan
pneumatic drills. Thousands of local workers and skilled tradesmen imported
from northern Morocco are still employed, almost fifteen years after the
Moroccan takeover, in building yet more roads, houses and hospitals for
indigenous ethnic Sahrawis and Moroccan settlers. King Hassan claims to
have historic royal rights over the former Spanish Sahara, but in the battle for
the hearts and minds of the Sahrawi people, his massive financial investment
is thought to be a worthwhile insurance premium to persuade waverers of
the advantages of being part of Morocco.

Three hundred miles east of the Moroccan-administered town of
Layounne, in the baking heat of the desert, exiled Polisario guerillas dismiss
all of the building work as an expensive waste of the king's money. In their
vast tent city, which they have called Layounne camp after the city which
they fled in 1976, the Polisario has set up schools, hospitals and even
vegetable gardens in the few places where water can be found. Both the

Polisario and the Moroccan authorities claim that a majority of the indigenous Sahrawis are on their side; the guerillas say that most will vote for independence when the United Nations organises a referendum, while King Hassan says a majority will opt for confirming the integration of the area into Morocco.

But before the UN sends in its election officials and military monitors, one rather basic question has to be solved, and that is agreeing on who has the right to vote. As in any guerilla war, many ethnic Sahrawis are displaced as refugees, but counting them in their remote camps is a relatively easy task compared with the thornier one of determining who has the right to vote. For example, the Polisario says it has 165,000 people in its camps. Morocco counters that the guerillas have less than 50,000. The Moroccan governor of the town of Layounne says he has 100,000 people living there. But Polisario counters that most of these are settlers from northern Morocco or people pretending to be Sahrawis in order to cheat their way into gaining a right to vote. An exasperated United Nations has therefore gone back to a census of Sahrawis conducted in 1974 by the Spanish colonial authorities, and although both sides have agreed to accept this census as a base, there are still wide differences as to how far the base can be altered.

But this numbers game could, in any case, be futile. The Polisario has insisted that, in order for a free and fair referendum to take place, the Moroccan authorities must first withdraw their troops and administration. But most foreigners that I have spoken to that have visited the Moroccan-administered towns of the Western Sahara conclude that King Hassan's agreeing to such a withdrawal is most unlikely. Apart from the massive financial investment that his government has made, and the tens of thousands of Moroccan soldiers and civil servants he has sent to live there, the king has invested much personal prestige in the area. Since the king is considered to be both the temporal and Islamic spiritual leader of Morocco, this prestige is considerable.

At a vast new public square in Layounne that is surrounded by gold-topped bandstands, the king has received the pledges of allegiance of ethnic Sahrawis loyal to him, pledges which the Polisario says were all either forced out of the Sahrawis by the Moroccans, or were simply disingenuous. All

Sahrawis, says the Polisario, want independence. But matters may not be as simple as the Polisario would like. It is clear that, in the town of Layounne, there are at least some ethnic Sahrawis who would vote, if they got a chance, with the king, and therefore in favour of integration with Morocco. Against this can be balanced the fact that, again and again through African history, most recently in Zimbabwe and Namibia, people have voted during independence referendums for the side which has been seen to fight for that independence. This is the one possible advantage that the Polisario has over the superior military might and financial resources of Morocco. When that possible advantage could be tested in a referendum seems to most observers to be a long way off.

Sierra Leone was the assembly point for a West African peace-keeping force that eventually intervened in the Liberian civil war. It has also been providing shelter for countless refugees. But the capital, Freetown, is not without problems of its own.

SIERRA LEONE'S CRUMBLING INFRASTRUCTURE

RICK WELLS   FREETOWN, SIERRA LEONE   20 JULY 1990

Quite a number of Sierra Leoneans told me they were pleased to hear the name of their capital Freetown in the world news again. Generally, they said, they felt ignored, as if no one really cared about their problems. That they do have problems is without doubt.

Take the capital itself. From a distance, spread out between rolling hills, covered with lush tropical vegetation, and palm-fringed sandy beaches, the rusting tin roofs and low colonial-style buildings of Freetown have all the vibrancy and colour of an African paradise. Close up though, the dream fades. The city's infrastructure has all but collapsed and Freetown has become one large shanty town. There are those, mostly expatriates and the wealthier classes, who retreat each day above the filth and squalor to their homes in an area called Hill Station, settled by the British in colonial times to escape the malaria-infested coastal flats. But the vast majority live in crowded, crumbling dwellings, without electricity or proper sanitation. In the mornings what looks like mist overlying the city is in fact the smoke from numerous wood fires as people cook and heat their water.

Someone told me the problem was so many people had come into

Freetown from the villages, bringing their village habits with them. But the truth is Freetown has little to offer them in the way of affordable amenities and they're just surviving the best they can. The Chairman of Freetown City Council, Alfred Akibo-Betts, who faces the formidable task of trying to sort out this mess, spoke to me from behind a large desk in a large room in City Hall that has "Mayor's Parlour" written above the door.

Like some big, bad wolf, capable of being both charming and ruthless at the same time, he said in a booming voice that what was needed was a change in attitude among Sierra Leoneans, more discipline, and above all patriotism. But what many ordinary citizens told me of, in no uncertain terms, was their complete loss of faith in their political leaders. Curiously, the President himself, an army man, Major General Joseph Saidu Momoh, is disarmingly honest about his government's failures. Indeed, two power cuts during my interview with him in State House seemed scarcely worth remarking on. I'm doing my best, he seemed to be saying, but clearly that isn't anywhere near good enough.

Nowhere is Sierra Leone's decline more obvious and tragic than in the field of education. The older generation, particularly the Creoles, the descendants of liberated former slaves who first settled in the colony in the late 18th century, are nostalgic for the days when Freetown was known as the Athens of West Africa. Although undoubtedly elitist and very British in outlook, the country's schools and university used to be the envy of many African countries. Now, after years of underfunding and neglect, they too are in a state of crisis. Most of last term was lost through strikes by teachers seeking better pay and conditions. Many parents, torn between support for the teachers and their children's needs, now have to face the possibility that the rising cost of exam fees will have put paid to their hopes for their children's education anyway. Ironically, one solution being put forward by the government is for private proprietors to take back the running of schools from the state. In some instances, this could mean a return to the old-style missionary school, but the question is whether things have actually got too bad for anyone to want to take them over.

Increasingly, Sierra Leoneans are talking about the need for change in the way they are governed as a way out of their problems. Inspired by the revolutions in Eastern Europe, the talk, as elsewhere in Africa, is of a return to a multi-party system of government, of democracy, and of the need to have "checks and balances" to counter the corruption that has stifled any attempts at effective government. Cynics, mostly out-of-work politicians who while away their time in the virtually defunct City Hotel, made famous by the writer Graham Greene in his book *The Heart of the Matter,* point out that Sierra Leone has tried most systems of government - multi-party, coalition, military and one-party - without success.

So maybe the big bad wolf was right. It's not so much the system as a change of attitude that's needed. The question is whether Sierra Leoneans have the will to do it themselves rather than wait for someone else, as in neighbouring Liberia, who would be prepared to tear the place apart before it could ever be rebuilt.

One of the great revolutionary figures of our time - Ahmed Ben Bella -
returned to Algeria in September after ten years of exile. He had led Algeria
to independence in 1962 and was overthrown as president three years
later. But the country he was returning to was now a very different one.

BEN BELLA: RETURN OF THE ALGERIAN LION

PETER HIETT   ALGIERS   2 OCTOBER 1990

I t was a distinctly undignified return for the man who had led his country
to independence. His first words back in Algeria were: "Du calme, du
calme" - not because the crowds on the dockside were wildly enthusiastic -
that would have been acceptable - even desirable - but because the scrum of
newsmen was pressing forward so strongly that he himself was immobilized,
stuck on the gangway of the ferry which had brought him home.

It took police and bodyguards the best part of a quarter of an hour to get
him inside the port's reception room. As it was, not all of his travelling party
made it. I heard one woman sobbing: "Let me in, let me in, I'm a relative!" -
on the wrong side of the reception room's door.

It was such a contrast to the early days back in the '60's, when millions
hung on his every word. Newly independent Algeria had won its freedom in
war, rather than around the negotiating table. Its sense of pride was
infectious. Its economy and society were run along impeccably left-wing
lines: the oil bonanza meant it could afford to do so. Successful, radical,
revolutionary Algeria symbolized everything that independence fighters
around the world aspired to, and the charismatic young Ben Bella

personified Algeria.

For him, the glory ended in 1965, when he was overthrown and replaced by the grim figure of his defence minister Hourari Boumedienne. Ben Bella stayed in prison for fourteen years until Boumedienne had died and his successor released him into closely-watched freedom. Eighteen months later he fled, vowing not to return until democracy reigned in Algeria.

In fact, Algeria is not quite there, though it is certainly on the road. Violent riots two years ago led to a series of reforms aimed at giving Algeria as western a system as possible. There are now more than twenty legal opposition parties, including Mr Ben Bella's own Movement for Democracy in Algeria, and the centralised controls are coming off the economy. But ordinary people are not yet feeling the benefit, and the government's reformist programme is provoking opposition across the political spectrum.

On the left, the trade unions and some others are criticising what they call the savage liberalism which is eroding job security and opening up the economy to foreigners. On the right, the Islamic Fundamentalists, who won the local and regional elections in June by a wide margin, criticise laxness and corruption which they lay at the door of the ruling FLN. The FLN itself is split between supporters of the reforms and those who want to return to the one-party state, and all that implies.

So it is to an Algeria fragmented as never before that Ahmed Ben Bella has returned, an Algeria trying painfully to shake off the past for which he himself is partly responsible. Many now look to him to put things right. To do that, he is first going to have to strengthen his own party. That will not be impossible: Ben Bella the political operator has not lost his skill; Ben Bella the orator is as powerful as ever. Many of the people who voted Fundamentalist in June did so mainly as a protest against the FLN. They may come over to him, especially as the Fundamentalists themselves are in some danger of splitting. He may also tap a reservoir of support from disgruntled elements in what is left of the FLN, and there is more support in his home region of Ouahran.

But will this be enough? There is a lot of competition on the Algerian political scene these days, the kind of open legal opposition in a free system he is not used to; and for many young Algerians who were not even born when he was president, Ben Bella is just another old man from the history books. Now in his seventies, he has lost the dynamism he once possessed, and at times seems ill.

Realistically, he cannot hope much for any kind of future, let alone one of leading his country again. But his opponents should not write him off too quickly. The French did so several times. They were wrong, as they found out to their cost. And in a political scene as fluid and complex as Algeria's almost anything can happen. The old lion may be enfeebled, but he still has teeth.

Elizabeth Blunt takes a look beyond the easy assumptions that are often made in the West about the social and economic roles of West African women.

WOMEN OF NIGERIA

ELIZABETH BLUNT   BAMAKO   16 DECEMBER 1989

I was chatting recently to a group of Nigerian women and I happened to ask one of them what she did for a living. She said she was a soap maker, producing the round balls of black soap which Nigerians believe is particulary good for the skin. And she said she also had a stall where she sold small bits and pieces - cigarettes, matches, and sweets - things like that. So I said, did that mean she wasn't a farmer? That brought a very indignant response: of course she had a farm, she said. She grew yams and cassava and most of the family's vegetables. I said that must keep her pretty busy; what did she do for pleasure and relaxation? Oh for relaxation, she said, she ran a nursery looking after under-threes. And as well as these four fairly full-time jobs, she obviously fitted in her housework and managed to be an active member of the local womens' self-help group, since that was how I had met her.

That woman wasn't unusual, either in Nigeria or anywhere else in West Africa. When I mentioned her to a Malian friend, she couldn't see the point of the story. Here it is normal for women to be both busy and productive. The Economic Commission for Africa states that women grow 80% of Africa's food. In parts of Ghana and Nigeria, women run the retail trade and virtually 100% of market traders are women. A BBC colleague who recently visited Nigeria for the first time said it was obvious to him what the women did, but he couldn't see what the men did all day...

I am a little ashamed to realise what Nigerians must have thought of the first European women who came to West Africa, many of them protected, idle, and dependent. I know they are shocked by the way European Law discriminated against women until very recently. Even in the Muslim north of Nigeria, where many women are still secluded in a form of purdah, they have always had the right to own their own land and to keep their own earnings. If a man needs some of his wives' money, he has to ask them nicely, and even then they don't have to give it to him.

Whatever else Nigerian women are, they are certainly never dependent. The whole notion of women as an asset and not a liability pervades traditional society. Take dowry, for instance - or, more properly speaking, bride-price. In south-eastern Nigeria, if a man wants to marry he often has to pay quite a large sum to the girl's parents to get her. But in Europe in the old days her father had to give a dowry with her, unless she was very beautiful, otherwise no husband would take her off his hands.

W ell, I know that I would rather be seen as an asset than a liability, although I do see that a bride-price does have its drawbacks. It is still common in poor families for a father to force his thirteen or fourteen year old daughter to marry, because he needs the money to put her younger brothers and sisters through school. Some families, having paid for a bride, clearly regard her as their property, to the extent that if her husband dies she still belongs to his family, and they expect their money back if she wants to leave them or to marry someone else.

Nigeria's modern institutions - largely British-inspired - often sit uneasily with this traditional viewpoint. In law, for instance, marriage ends with the death of one of the partners; there is no question of being married to the family. Development projects, often funded and organised by people brought up in a European tradition, can easily fall into the trap of assuming that men are the producers, and women the passive consumers of development - people who need to be given things like water pumps and health centres. This may have worked during Nigeria's oil boom, but nowadays if Nigerian women are expected to wait until someone gives them what they need, they are clearly never going to get it.

NORTH AMERICA

General Noriega was finally prised from the Vatican embassy in Panama after days of negotiations, accompanied by an almost continual bombardment of high decibel rock music. In the United States there was jubilation that the aims of 'Operation Just Cause' - the code name for the American invasion of Panama - had been achieved.

THE MORAL CASE FOR OPERATION 'JUST CAUSE'

STEPHEN JESSEL   WASHINGTON D.C.   6 JANUARY 1990

L ess than an hour after General Noriega's surrender and departure as a prisoner apparently in chains on an American Air Force plane bound for Miami, President Bush addressed the nation. The four aims of the invasion had been achieved, he said: the safeguarding of the lives of American citizens; helping restore democracy to Panama, the protection of the integrity of the Panama Canal Treaties; the bringing to justice of Noriega.

The United States, said Mr Bush, had used its resources in a manner consistent with political, diplomatic and moral principles. There are not many voices raised in the US to contradict him. The invasion was a wildly popular move with, I would guess, 90% of Americans, and from what I could see in the western-most province of Panama, with about that proportion of Panamanians. At a bound, mild-mannered, bespectacled Mr Bush has shed his over-cautious wimp image and emerged in his super-president costume.

The United States military establishment is beside itself with glee. Some of the comment would suggest that the attack by 24,000 well-armed, well-equipped American troops against a smaller, less well-armed force from a base inside Panama itself was a feat of arms unparalleled since Agincourt. Within minutes of Bush's brief speech, a caller was exulting on a late-night television talk show that the ghost of Vietnam had finally been exorcised. Other callers took up the theme. Few tears should be shed for Noriega - a corrupt and brutal thug who terrorized and impoverished his country. Yet even the most exuberant of parties can be followed by hangovers, and though there are very few at the moment, some voices are asking awkward questions. Indeed, there is reason to challenge almost every assertion made by Mr Bush.

Noriega is indeed in American hands, though whether in the present lynch-mob climate he will get justice in the form of a fair trial is another question altogether. No serious evidence has been produced that the operations of the Panama Canal were ever in danger. As for the restoration of democracy, the new Panamian president almost certainly did win last year's aborted elections; but the manner of his swearing-in - on a military base belonging to a foreign power - was not an auspicious start to his career. For the time being at least, the United States is plainly running Panama. Mr Bush's words about the protection of American lives - a reference to the murder by Panamanian troops of an American lieutenant which was the immediate cause of the invasion - have to be contrasted with the extreme caution of the Administration's reaction to the murder of an American nun in neighbouring Nicaragua. Circumstances there suggested that the American-backed Contras might well have been responsible.

All these points can, of course, be disputed. Noriega *will get* a fair trial; democracy *will* be restored in due course; Noriega's conduct *did* endanger the Canal treaties; the killing of Lieutenant Paz - 'peace' in Spanish - could be firmly attributed to Noriega's men. But there are many other questions too. Two weeks after the invasion, the Unites States, which can normally tell you how many rounds of ammunition it has captured, cannot - or will not - give a figure for the number of Panamanians killed in the invasion, partly as a result of indiscriminate use of heavy weapons in built-up areas. Estimates start at 250, and some go a good deal higher. The conduct of the military also provokes a number of questions. They ignored the diplomatic status of the Nicaraguan Ambassador's residence, for which Bush half-apologised; searched other Nicaraguan diplomatic residences; raided the offices of the Spanish news agency; and according to some reports, carted off files on political parties.

Mr Bush spoke of the political, diplomatic and moral principles of the United States. These presumably include the rule of law, but even at this stage it is not evident at all what the legal basis for the American action was. A country of 250 million people can hardly plead self-defence against a state of two million people separated by several hundred miles. Diplomatically, the affair was hardly a triumph. The vote in the Organisation of American States went against the United States; in the United Nations General Assembly it was 75/20 against, with even some NATO countries voting against or abstaining. Relations with Nicaragua, already dreadful, have deteriorated further. And the Sandinistas now have a plausible case for calling off next month's elections, given the presence in the neighbouring state of several thousand troops belonging to its bitterest enemy - an enemy which has intervened in the affairs of Panama and the Philippines in a matter of weeks.

Morally? Well, Noriega may be a swine, but he was a swine even when he was on the CIA payroll. He is a bad man, but there are worse... and no country which supports Pol Pot and is courting the old men who sent the tanks into Tiananmen Square should concentrate too much of its case on morality.

*In the four turbulent years since the collapse of the Duvalier dictatorship
in the Caribbean republic of Haiti, governments have come and gone at a
dizzying pace. Amid the chaos, one of Haiti's most beautiful landmarks,
the Grand Hotel Oloffson, went out of business for a time. However, such
is the charm of the former presidential palace that its new owners
reopened it despite the lack of custom.*

CONSTANT WITNESS TO HAITI'S NIGHTMARE

ALAN TOMLINSON   PORT AU PRINCE   20 MARCH 1990

The number of empty tables on the Oloffson verandah has become a
barometer of Haiti's political climate. In the dark days of Papa Doc
Duvalier and the Ton Ton Macoute, the hotel's former owner, the late Al Seitz
who reputedly won the place in a poker game, would sit here under the
potted palms and regale Graham Greene with the woes of running a hotel
without guests. Seitz's stories were Greene's inspiration for 'The Comedians'.

Today, it is the new owner, Richard Morse, who balefully eyes the
newshounds who flock here for the latest chapter of Haiti's recurring political
nightmare. He knows that the horror stories they write will keep his regular
clients away for months. The violence of the past four years caused the
Oloffson to close for a time, when Seitz's widow Suzanne gave up the
struggle to meet her rising bills. She watched the famous artists and actors
who were once her regulars slowly drift away, leaving only their memories

171

on the suites and cottages dotted among the tropical shrubbery. Noel Coward and Lillian Hellman from one generation, Mick Jagger from another. With their passing, the throngs who came to rub shoulders with them also thinned out.

A hardier band of Oloffson addicts lingers on. They're drawn here by the enigmatic charm of Haiti and by the illustrious Victorian building that has been a theatre box on an awesome historical drama. It was built at the turn of the century by an ill-fated Haitian president, who was later torn to pieces on the streets below by an angry mob. The rambling wooden mansion rises above a jungle of swaying palms like a childhood fantasy: a towering pile of turrets, towers, balconies and lacy gingerbread grillwork held together by layers of ageing white paint. As Greene wrote, "It has the air at night of a Charles Addams house in a number of 'The New Yorker'. You expect a witch to open the door to you, or a maniac butler with a bat dangling from the chandelier behind him."

After the first owner's unfortunate demise, American marines invaded Haiti and used the mansion as a hospital during their occupation until 1934. It was then that Oloffson, a Norwegian sea-captain, turned it into a hotel. Against all the odds, as political violence continues to keep tour companies away from Haiti, former reggae musician Richard Morse has rescued the place from permanent closure and restored its quirky glory. To the wickerwork furniture and enormous mahogany beds, he has added a new collection of primitive Haitian art to replace the one the widow Seitz auctioned off. In a studio near the car park, a local craftsman sews sequins onto magical voodoo flags, while on Monday nights the hotel chambermaids and the owner's beautiful wife Lunise transform themselves into voodoo dancers under the expert choreography of Morse's famous Haitian mother, retired cabaret artiste Emerante de Pradines - or Emmy to her friends.

But those of us who still dine here regularly under the ceiling fans on the wide verandah have often been treated to an even more startling cabaret. The hotel has a commanding view of the national palace, where the din of battle regularly signals a change of government. One recent coup attempt sent tracers screaming into the night sky over the hotel roof. The band played on. At breakfast, one of Haiti's most irrepressible characters, the newspaper columnist and art collector Aubelin Jolicoeur, is usually on hand to explain how things turned out. Greene immortalised him in 'The Comedians' as Petit Pierre, the dapper social gadfly with the silver-topped cane and the uncanny knack of surviving the political ups and downs that bring such disaster to others. Auby, as he is known in real life, was a minister himself for a few weeks in one short-lived government, but these days, like his host Richard Morse, he finds he has a lot more time on his hands for a quiet chat over backgammon with the handful of guests brave enough to keep coming to Haiti.

The faithful few fill the hours lounging by the swimming pool, wondering if tomorrow, as in Greene, the Interior Minister's body might be found beneath the diving platform. Or at sunset, we gather for rum punch at the bar to keep an eye on the sagging wooden ceiling, where the Anne Bancroft Suite constantly threatens to collapse onto the piano.

Every day in New York City thirty people die of AIDS or are told they have the virus. The shock felt over the relentless spread of the epidemic is in strange contrast to New York's traditional belief in itself as the ultimate city, as Martin Lumb discovered.

AIDS IN NEW YORK

MARTIN LUMB   NEW YORK CITY   12 APRIL 1990

I t is hard to dent the confidence of such a unique and vibrant place as New York, but the fear of AIDS has succeeded in a way that nothing has done since the Depression. Rich and poor, young and old alike tell you of that fear, not just over what might happen to them, but what is happening to their city. In downtown New York, Greenwich Village has long been the epitome of much that is youthful, stylish and outrageous about the city. It is ironic that the Village is now also the location of the only shelter specifically for homeless people with AIDS.

I spoke there with Michael - young, well-educated and prosperous before the symptoms emerged a year ago and grew rapidly worse. Speech was exhausting for him, but he wanted to tell me of the full life he'd led before he got sick, and his fondness for New York. It was easy to tell how well he would have fitted into the colourful street life of Greenwich Village, not far from the bed that now he rarely leaves. His close neighbour was Gwen, a poor woman who drifted to New York City, got AIDS through injecting drugs, went blind and is now very sick. In a dignified and unreproachful way she too told her sad story.

AIDS is cutting through a generation of New Yorkers like Michael and Gwen with horrifying effect - it is the leading cause of death in men and women between their mid-twenties and mid-thirties, the leading killer of babies, and the third-highest killer in the population as a whole. But if the people sick with AIDS in New York now are only the tip of the iceberg, the disease itself is only one manifestation of an even bigger problem facing the city - that of poverty.

It is among the intravenous drug users, many of them from disadvantaged minority groups, people like Gwen, living in the slums and ghettos or in the open street, that the disease is spreading. The gay community, which suffered the initial brunt of the epidemic, has changed its way of life and now the number of homosexuals getting the disease is levelling off. That's the only reason for optimism in this depressing picture; it seems the message has got through in the gay community, but hope for the likes of Gwen is still a long way off.

New York desperately needs tax dollars from the rest of the country where AIDS is not so much of a priority - New York is home to nearly a quarter of all the AIDS patients in the United States. Last year it cost nearly a thousand million dollars to care for them; by 1992 it is reckoned the cost will be double that amount - all that from a city that's broke. Declare it a disaster zone, pleaded one activist I spoke to, arguing that if two hundred people died in an earthquake, federal money would pour in.

A IDS will soon be the worst epidemic of the century in New York, passing the twenty-odd thousand deaths from an influenza outbreak around 1920. Not since the terrible epidemics of smallpox and cholera in the nineteenth century has a single disease had such an impact. At the most conservative estimate, there are now 125,000 New Yorkers carrying the virus and many of them don't know it.

The city is fighting back in a number of ways that seem to bring out the best and the worst in its multi-sided personality. Compassion grows as the facts about AIDS become more widely known and more people know someone with the disease. At the same time, according to the gay community, bigotry is on the increase. Modern New York was built by people whose very arrival here was proof that they could triumph over adversity, but if their descendants are to beat this latest and most dangerous threat they'll need more than their own native resourcefulness – and that growing compassion.

On the eve of his departure from the United States, Stephen Jessel made a list of the best things about the country which included, in no particular order: the breathtaking National Parks, the Constitution, shirts, the interstate highway system, motels, San Francisco, Chesapeake Bay crabs - and baseball.

THE PULL
OF BASEBALL

STEPHEN JESSEL   WASHINGTON D.C.   30 JULY 1990

I t is a shame that given the choice between the two national American sports -American football and baseball - the British have elected to squander their enthusiasm on the former, a dull, violent, brutish affair, full of wild swirls of incomprehensible action followed by interminable pauses and played by mastodons in armour.

The nation that gave the world cricket should adore baseball -and indeed the two games have a certain spiritual similarity. Both pit a man with a ball against a man with a bat. Both put a premium on skill in running, catching and throwing. Both are a treasure chest for those who love statistics and averages.

Baseball, as everyone knows, is a fancy form of rounders, though maybe one should not say so too loudly in the cheap seats of Yankee Stadium. Runs are scored when players make their way round the four bases, generally by hitting the ball so that they reach first or second base before the throw from the fielder arrives there, and making further progress on fair hits by other batters. But within this relatively simple framework, what exquisite subtleties lurk; what splendid athleticism displays itself. The art of stealing a base for example - that is, running from one base to the next, usually while the pitcher is preparing to throw, and aiming to beat the throw from the pitcher or from the catcher, who is the masked figure corresponding to a wicket keeper squatting behind the batter.

To see Mr Ricky Henderson of the Oakland Athletics, by some way the best team in baseball, sprint the 30 yards from one base to the next, arriving in a slide and a cloud of dust as the throw comes whistling in, is as exhilarating a sight as you might wish for. And yet - and here is the joy of it - you don't have to be Mr Henderson. At least two men in their early to mid-forties are playing top-level baseball, and playing it better than ever. There are some players, usually pitchers, whose substantial midriffs, encased in the traditional tight uniforms, display evidence of many long hours communing with another sort of pitcher, this time full of beer, and by the look of it, substantial quantities of pizza too.

Baseball is a game full of moments of great drama, as when a team deliberately allows opponents onto all the bases. The risk is that the batter will hit a fair ball, allowing up to four runs to score. But he may hit in such a way that in a lightning relay of the ball the fielding team may get two or even three of the base runners out, and after three outs in an inning, that inning is over. And a team that seems hopelessly beaten three quarters of the way through may rally in the 7th or 8th or 9th inning and start scoring.

I f anything is wrong with baseball, it is that it has become the pet of some American intellectuals who have taken to finding truths about the American and human condition in what is at heart just a very good game. But that is not baseball's fault, and it has many virtues. For one thing, it appeals - unlike American football - outside North America. The Japanese and the Cubans play baseball; the Taiwanese and the Nicaraguans love the game; and in America's slow march to racial equality, a march no European is in much of a position to criticise, baseball has played a big part. Jackie Robinson was the first black player in the major leagues in the 1940s. There are two black managers, including Frank Robinson, the unfailingly amiable - perhaps a little too amiable - manager of the Baltimore Orioles. The type of crude racial abuse heard at British soccer grounds has no place in stadiums here, which are in any case far more people-friendly and family-orientated than British football grounds.

Americans are proud of having invented baseball in the mid-19th century, and so they should be. Far be it from me to mention that in 'Northanger Abbey' by Jane Austen - started 1797, published 1819 - there is mention of this all-American pastime.

LATIN AMERICA

December	14 1989	Patricio Aylwin elected President of Chile, ending 16 years of Military Rule
December	17 1989	Fernando Collor de Mello elected President of Brazil, ending 29 years of Military Rule
December	27 1989	US invades Panama, General Noriega topped
January	4 1990	General Noriega captured. Taken to US for trial
February	1 1990	Diplomatic relations re-established between Britain and Argentina
February	26 1990	Sandinistas lose Nicaraguan elections to Violeta Chamorro

An unchecked Gold Rush has brought more than 45,000 Gold Prospectors to the lands of 9,000 Yannomami Indians in Brazil's Northern Amazon region. It's been disastrous, both for the Environment and for the Indians, whose very survival is now threatened.

GOLD FEVER, INDIAN FEVER

JAN ROCHA   SAO PAULO   9 DECEMBER 1989

The hospital for Indians in Boa Vista was crammed full of maleria cases. Men and boys; women and babies lay in hammocks, sick and listless. Rubbish lay about on the dirt floor. A nurse in a Snoopy tee-shirt walked around with a tray of medicines, barking out names. "Hey, grandad, come and get your medicine!" she called to an old man. But most of the Yanomami Indians don't speak or understand Portuguese, and they don't recognise the names given to them on admission to the hospital, because their real names are secret and can't be spoken by anyone else. Nor are the children any more at ease out of their environment: three small boys sat on a bench looking at a colour television set. It was tuned to a children's programme in Rio, 3,000 miles to the south, but it might as well have been coming from the moon.

Doctor Jose Pereira comes in for a few hours every morning. He is the only doctor for all the 35,000 Indians in the state. he said the Yanomami used to be happy and healthy. They lived on a subsistence diet, but it was enough. After the gold prospectors came, the game was frightened away by the noise, and the fish have disappeared. The Indians have stopped planting because they are bewildered, they don't know what is happening to them. They now depend on the prospectors for food handouts. In the hospital, which is run by the National Indian Bureau, the only food available is the Brazilian staple diet - beans and rice. Even though the Indians are not used to this food, that is all they get.

Every five minutes or so, an aeroplane droned overhead on its way to or from the 100 or so airstrips that have been slashed out of the forest inside Yanomami land. Nobody bothered to look up. Before the gold rush began three years ago, the only access was by river, and two or three airstrips used by the Indian Bureau authorities and by the military. Now the prospectors have scattered throughout the Yanomami's mountainous forested territory, tearing away at the riverbanks, cutting down trees and throwing mercury into the rivers.

Their only communication is by radio. I went to the radio station in Boa Vista which transmits over 200 messages a day to them:

"Attention Adam - better known as Old Negro in the Mucajai. Your wife says she's had the baby; it's a boy and they're both well and you must send some gold."

"Attention Ernandes, better known as Rich. Your wife Olga says the man you sent the gold with didn't deliver it. She doesn't know what to do and she's losing patience."

"Attention Pedro at the Swollen Feet Airstrip. Let me know if you've got the revolver I sent you."

Boa Vista is the capital of Roraima in Brazil's northern Amazon. It used to be a small quiet town of tree-lined streets, but since the gold rush began the population has trebled, and cases of robbery, violence and murder have multiplied. After a month in the wild, the prospectors fly back into town with their precious grams of gold dust, which they keep inside small plastic medicine bottles. The taxis at the airport charge them one gram of gold for the ride into town.

In the Street of the Gold Buyers, lined with identical shops, I watched a prospector called Raimundo carefully pour out his gold-dust - 35 grams of it - onto the scales to be weighed. He told me he had worked 48 days to get those 35 grams, risking malaria, attack by vampire bats, sleeping in a hammock under a tree. But it earned him ten times as much as he could earn as a labourer, so it was worth it.

Altogether about two or three tonnes of gold a month are produced by the prospectors. For the Yanomami, the gold of course spells disaster, possibly the end. A doctor who investigated the situation recently said that without urgent measures, the result could amount to genocide.

Belatedly, the Brazilian government has now announced an emergency medical plan to try and put an end to the malaria, the venereal diseases, the tuberculosis and malnutrition. But they still hesitate to remove the prospectors because they don't know what to do with 45,000 rootless, gold-hungry men. Until they do this, the prospectors will go on spreading death and destruction in their search for the precious dust.

In late February voters in Nicaragua flocked to the polls to inflict a crushing defeat on the Sandinistas. Robin Dilks looked at some of the lessons of these elections and what they meant for Central America.

PROSPECTS FOR NICARAGUA

ROBIN DILKS   MANAGUA   2 MARCH 1990

S andinista-watchers have all along credited them with being flexible and adroit, experts at seizing the initiative and staying in front, and profiting from the divisions among their enemies, whether in jungle camps, diplomatic gatherings or in Washington. So their election defeat still needs some explaining.

Part of the reason is that economic and military pressure had worn down their popularity. After ten years the glow of revolution had long since dimmed; people were weary of war and penury, and wanted a change, any change. All the government had done was to survive. But when the Sandinistas agreed to the elections last year, just as economic austerity was biting, they realised all this. They ran a thorough, well-organised campaign to build on the 30% bedrock support usually credited to them. Daniel Ortega criss-crossed the country tirelessly appearing at rallies. There were fireworks, shows, all the gimmicks of a determined campaign. The defeat was all the more surprising considering the reach of the Sandinista Front organisation. The correspondent of the Financial Times called it "an apparatus which extends from a vastly expanded public service through the trade unions, youth and women's organisations, down to neighbourhood committees, all of which rests on the pillars of the armed forces, the police and the security services."

At opposition rallies, ending military conscription was the promise that raised the biggest cheers. Mothers as well as young conscripts hated it. Daniel Ortega was hinting he would relax it. "If they do," declared Violeta Chamorro, "it will be because of pressure from the opposition." The word was that Ortega had an announcement ready for the big closing rally four days before the elections. But he didn't make it.

One source with multiple contacts inside the upper echelons of the Front suggested that on the night the announcement was due, Mr Ortega was so impressed with the vast crowd mobilised by the party machine that he decided to withdraw the concession on the draft at the last minute. A large part of that crowd trailed home very disgruntled, angry enough to swell the protest vote for the opposition, even though few of them really believed they would overthrow the revolution.

If this is true, it would mean that Ortega made a monumental mistake because he was fooled by his own propaganda. It is a blunder with a sobering message for many other Latin American politicians: never underestimate your electorate, don't rely on the protection of propaganda and populism any more, it no longer works on its own: the issues really do count.

If the tricky transition is accomplished in Nicaragua, this unexpected result would almost complete a sea-change in Central America. Since November 1989, new leaders much more friendly to the United States have been chosen in Honduras, Costa Rica and now in Nicaragua, and one was imposed in Panama. El Salvador moved sharply to the right last year. Guatemala could follow suit. The focus of those regional summits is expected to switch from building peace to a much more concerted programme of economic revival.

But aid workers and some in the international agencies are worried that private businesses will be promoted at the expense of social programmes. They refer almost wistfully to the two great achievements of the Sandinistas, in their early years of government - teaching Nicaraguans to read and write, and vastly improving children's health. The aid experts further fear that with political and economic attention now concentrated on Eastern Europe, and with Central America still unable to stand on its own feet, the 'backyard' will again be neglected - and its political stability will be short-lived.

One of the biggest electoral upheavals in Latin America this year was the unexpected defeat of the acclaimed Novelist, Maria Vargas Llosa, in the Peruvian elections after a second round of voting. Before the first round, Robin Dilks sent this report.

POLITICAL EARTHQUAKES IN PERU

ROBIN DILKS   LIMA   20 APR 1990

As well as being a brilliant novelist, Mario Vargas Llosa has been one of the best interpreters of Latin America's idiosyncratic ways to the outside world.

He wrote an essay three years ago analysing the cultural origins of the region's confusion between fiction and fact, between illusion and reality. He traced this back to the suppression of literature during colonial rule by Spain. He argued that with no formal outlet for the imagination, the habit of making up and telling stories became so deeply embedded in everyday life that people lost the ability to tell the difference. In literary circles the phenomenon is called 'the revenge of the novel'. In its final stages, Peru's election campaign had a clear script, which could have been entitled 'The revenge of the novelist'.

Mr Vargas Llosa had interrupted his literary career to enter the sordid world of politics. He led the opinion polls in an otherwise not very distinguished field of presidential candidates. He shares Mrs Thatcher's conviction that too much state power - especially over the economy - stifles individual initiative and freedom. Mr Vargas Llosa - heading an uneasy alliance of conservative parties - looked like winning the elections and embarking on root-and-branch reforms: privatisation, dropping import barriers, dropping subsidies, balancing the books.

To outsiders, the plot looked consistent, and workable. A chain reaction of free-market reforms - from Mexico to Argentina - had fizzed through Latin America in the last 18 months. Mr Vargas Llosa had international prestige as well as novelty to offer the voters. But early support for him started to slide. His opponents hit out at his capitalist shock treatment plan - was more unemployment and poverty really right for a country like Peru where at least a quarter of the population is already destitute? Secondly, even conservatives here admit that the novelist fell among thieves. He became too closely identified with some of the discredited old guard on the right. His candidacy lost its gloss: those who had scrambled on board all but sank the vessel. The main beneficiary was not the centre-left ruling party, known as APRA, which won the presidency for Mr Alan Garcia five long years ago.

Nor did the divided Peruvian left reap any political dividends. Instead, around a third of the voters or 3 million Peruvians flocked to an even newer newcomer, Mr Alberto Fujimori. His parents arrived in Peru from Japan in 1930. He looks professional and efficient and talks common sense. Who knows - went the rumours - he might be the channel for massive Japanese investment. Unofficial results suggest that Mr Fujimori may end up only narrowly behind Mr Vargas Llosa - whose 30-35% showing, while remarkable in itself, now looks more like a defeat. These two political novices should be contesting a second round of voting in the coming weeks.

But Mr Vargas Llosa doesn't want that. He says Peru's recession and guerilla war against the Sendero Luminoso (Shining Path) insurgents demand quick answers. The story so far is an improbable one - no author could have devised a character to match Mr Fujimori. But behind the drama and surprise, the political horizon is cloudy. The voters have rejected worn-out political models, but they haven't defined a clear alternative. Peruvians are apprehensive, hoping that the thickening political plot can be quickly resolved and without a bitter sequel.

On May Day in Cuba, three and a half million people - a third of the island's population - went on to the streets in what the authorities claimed was a massive demonstration in support of the revolution. But Fidel Castro has been profoundly shaken by the historic changes in the Soviet Union.

RETURN TO HAVANA

JOHN RETTIE   HAVANA   3 MAY 1990

I n the run-up to May Day, processions of cars and vans drove around the streets of Havana, calling on people with loud-hailers and stirring, patriotic posters to make sure they attended the demonstration in Revolution Square. The most stirring poster I saw was of a scantily-clad, dusky-skinned maiden with the most aggressively curvaceous posterior your imagination could invent. "Purely Cuban!" was the patriotic slogan that accompanied her. In non-communist western countries, this would have been angrily denounced by the mildest of progressives as outrageously sexist. But Cubans, women as well as men, socialists and non-socialists alike, are intensely, even brazenly, proud of the beauty of their "mulatas", as they call the mixed race lovelies who adorn their island.

Indeed, the dreary, monotonous and rather puritanical version of socialism developed in the Soviet Union, and known as Marxism-Leninism, always seemed hopelessly out of place in this tropical Caribbean island inhabited by a people of mixed Spanish and African stock. Socialism perhaps, if their revolutionary hero, Fidel Castro, said so. But Marxism-Leninism, as developed by Stalin and his successors, has proved to be a failed experiment even in the Soviet Union and eastern Europe. How does it survive in Cuba?

It survives, less changed than anywhere but Albania and North Korea, because of Fidel Castro and the unwavering support of the Soviet Union. But is Castro still the Cuban people's hero, and is Moscow's support still unwavering? If the answers to these questions are no, are Castro and his regime doomed to collapse like those of eastern Europe, or to be voted out of office like the Sandinistas in Nicaragua?

To some people the answers to these questions are simple. The Cuban exiles in Miami, for example, are convinced that Fidel's days are numbered. Lawyers among them are getting rich drawing up legal documents for their well-to-do clients to recover property nationalised after the Cuban revolution 31 years ago. This is more than a little premature, not to say an advanced case of wishful thinking. Others in the United States and elsewhere see Cuba being abandoned by a Soviet Union increasingly irritated by Castro's unwillingness to change, and by the growing strain of an aid burden on the shaky Soviet economy. After successfully forcing the Sandinista regime off the Nicaraguan stage by persistent economic, diplomatic and military pressure, some elements of the Bush administration appear to believe that such pressure will eventually dispose of Castro as well.

From inside Cuba, none of these views looks in the least realistic. There is no visible rival to Fidel Castro, and there are not going to be free elections, as there were in Nicaragua. Nor is the Soviet Union about to abandon Cuba, despite much grumbling about Cuban inefficiency and waste - grumbling fully matched, incidentally, by Cuban complaints of the poor quality of Soviet equipment. Castro had certainly displayed some nervousness about such a possibility. In February and March he staged an experiment in the western Pinar del Rio province, obscurely described as "a special period in times of peace". The idea was to see how they could manage in an emergency situation in which Soviet oil supplies were cut off. Wood was burned instead of oil or electricity in forges, oxen were used instead of tractors on the land, and manual instead of electric hoists in building works.

But these signs of incipient panic subsided in April after a visit by the deputy Soviet prime minister, Mr Leonid Abalkin, who visited Cuba for talks on this year's trade and aid package. Mr Abalkin made clear that their mutual trade was of great benefit to the Russians too. How, after all, would Moscow find hard currency to buy the sugar, nickel and citrus fruits they get from Cuba? The Cubans have also been told that Soviet military aid will also be maintained, and matched to the pressure exerted by the United States.

But all that does not mean that there is nothing to worry Castro. Before the changes in eastern Europe and Nicaragua, Cubans had for some time been asking themselves what would happen after Fidel. Now many are asking themselves what will happen during Fidel's time. Unassailable though his structural position may be, Castro has understood that Cuban society is seized of a deep malaise. His long-standing efforts at "rectification" have had no impact on the appalling inefficiency of a highly centralised economy, which his allies are now abandoning. He seems to have understood the need for far-reaching political changes, and has launched a nation-wide grassroots discussion, in preparation for next year's fourth congress of the Communist Party.

B ut the first problem is that many people cannot believe they can speak freely after so many years of warnings against counter-revolutionary views. The second is the question of whether Fidel Castro himself, at 63, is too old to change his views - though some believe he'll be as flexible as need be to save his revolution. The third, and perhaps most vital question, is whether Washington is yet ready to ease its pressure and allow Cuba to relax, in the interests of a political compromise. With so much political machismo on both sides, that certainly can't be taken for granted, and the long-term question mark over the Cuban revolution remains.

Over the past 30 years, the Cuban government has spent huge sums out of its scarce resources on creating what is probably the Third World's best health service. But now, with the economy in crisis and a question mark over Soviet aid, Cuba is taking a new interest in such alternative medicines as acupuncture and homeopathy.

ALTERNATIVE MEDICINE COMES TO CUBA

JOHN RETTIE   HAVANA   8 MAY 1990

S o effective has Cuba's health programme been that it's one of the few Third World nations whose population suffers from the kind of maladies that plague industrialised states - like heart disease, for example - rather than those characteristic of tropical countries. In fact, you can even get a heart transplant in Havana at one of the world's most advanced medical units.

Many people think this has all gone much too far in what's still, after all, a poor country, revolutionary or not. Not long ago, for example, the Cubans bought a highly sophisticated laser scanner, believed to have cost about two million dollars in scarce hard currency. The point is that after the revolution, the Cubans wanted to show that with a socialist government in charge, they could be among the world's leaders in medicine - orthodox western medicine, that is. At an exhibition of national achievements at a congressional meeting two years ago, a slogan for action over the medical section proclaimed: "To become a world medical power".

But under the impact of Cuba's deepening economic crisis, these grandiose ideas are beginning to change. For a year or two now, one of the world's leading practitioners of natural medicine, Professor Anton Jayasuriya of Sri Lanka, has had frequent invitations to Cuba, where he has had several meetings with Fidel Castro himself. As a result of these contacts, the Professor was invited by the health ministry to hold one of his regular international congresses in Havana. Arranged by his Colombo-based organisation *Medicina Alternativa,* these congresses are held in different parts of the world, to enable healers of various specialities to attend without spending too much time or money spanning the globe. The congress in Havana was the first in Latin America, and attracted participants from all over the continent - although two came from as far as China.

C uba's interest in alternative medicine for its own people only partly explains its invitation to *Medicina Alternativa.* Although he never expresses political opinions, Professor Jayasuriya's message is one with which a committed revolutionary like Fidel Castro is very happy to be associated. He is sharply critical of international drugs companies, for example, which he says exert excessive influence over both the World Health Organisation (WHO) and the Nobel Prize Institute. He accuses the WHO of paying only lip service to developing traditional medicines, and he has quarrelled with the Nobel Prize Institute because of its refusal to include practitioners of alternative medicine among candidates for the prize. In fact, the Professor says, the winner is usually a biochemist rather than a medical practitioner, and he's now asking for it to be called "the prize for allopathic medicine".

In a further counter-attack, *Medicina Alternativa* is to ask the United Nations to declare 1992 the Year of Complementary Medicines, and this too has enthusiastic Cuban support. As Professor Jayasuriya points out, more than half the world's people are treated with alternative forms of medicine, if only because nothing else is available. But as a doctor who qualified in orthodox medicine in London and Edinburgh, as well as in acupuncture in China, he insists he has no bias against any kind of medicine. He himself comes from a long line of ayurvedic healers in Sri Lanka, and his aim is that all forms of healing should be integrated by the end of the century. The professor claims that more and more young doctors of orthodox medicine all over the world are beginning to learn alternative forms of healing, which aim to treat a patient as a whole person, rather than to attack the specific disease by prescribing pills or wielding the surgeon's knife. There was much discussion at the congress of investigations into a homeopathic vaccine against AIDS, known as Aidinum, though it still exists only in experimental form.

The Cubans were delighted when Professor Jayasuriya described his message as revolutionary, even though it was a very different kind of revolution that he had in mind. But there was clearly a meeting of minds between two larger-than-life characters, both of whom feel they have a major world role to play in their chosen fields.

In Panama the US military appears to be expanding its role after American troops invaded the country to remove General Manuel Noriega from power. New anti-drug agreements have been signed with the US-backed government, and American troops have mounted operations in remote parts of the Panamanian jungle. David Adams spent five days in the rain forests of the Darien on the trail of the GI's.

DERRING-DO IN THE DARIEN

DAVID ADAMS   PANAMA CITY   20 MAY 1990

A good friend and colleague called me the other day. "There are GI's in the jungle," he said. "Let's go and look for them."
Evidence of American troops in the Panamanian countryside is not new here. But the area we were to visit, the rain forest of the Darien, on the border with Colombia, is a sensitive area where the Americans were not known to be operating.

The Darien is a region that has enticed many before now. The sixteenth century Spanish conquistadores searched there for gold. The British poet, John Keats, was inspired to write of Cortes, standing looking at the Pacific, "Silent, upon a peak in Darien."

In the late 17th century, William Patterson, founder of the Bank of England, established the disastrous colony of New Edinburgh, believing the Darien to be what he called "the door of the Seas, the key of the universe." The venture ruined the country's finances, and turned out to be one of the last acts of Scottish independence. Later the Americans explored the Darien believing it to be the narrowest part of the Central American isthmus and therefore the logical point to build the Panama Canal. The jungle got the better of them, too.

193

Today, the Darien remains wild and remote. The Pan-American highway stops at the edge of the Darien National Park, one of the world's largest nature reserves. All travel is by light aircraft, canoe or on foot. Its inaccessibility has made it a haven for smuggling. In 1984, the Colombian drug barons built a large cocaine processing laboratory there. Pablo Escobar, the Colombian drug kingpin, is reported to have a retreat in the forest on the Colombian side. Colombian and Panamanian guerillas are rumoured to operate in the area.

American officials say US troops are not involved in border security patrols or anti-narcotics operations in the Darien. If American soldiers go there at all it is only on what are called 'routine training exercises'.

The interest of my colleague and I was first aroused when we came across plastic wrappers from American military rations. Known as MRE's or 'Meals Ready to Eat', we found them littering a forest trail that led us across the border into Colombia.

However, our expectations were soon doused. At one meal halt, our Indian guide proceeded to pull from his rucksack an MRE packet containing Menu Number X, Frankfurters with Bean Component, which he greedily began to devour.

I t turned out that following last December's invasion, the Americans sent emergency food supplies to the Darien consisting mainly of MRE's. They appear to be regarded as quite a delicacy by the local population who are more used to a diet of iguana, toucan and cassava.

But peasants we spoke to on the forest paths did tell us stories of American soldiers on patrol nearby. In one case, we were told by a frightened peasant how he had been stopped at gunpoint by soldiers the day before. Under the muzzle of an M-16 rifle, he was questioned about his work, his papers were checked and his bags searched. They were looking for drugs and guns, he said.

It was the sight of American military Black Hawk helicopters that eventually led us to what we were looking for: a small camp site complete with satellite communications, beside a small civilian airstrip. American soldiers were deflating three French-made zodiac dinghies. After some hesitation they told us they were members of a 40-man elite Special Forces team. They were on a five-day mission, investigating reports of drug-trafficking and guerilla activity along the border. When their commanding officer appeared, he was visibly upset to find his men talking to reporters. He ordered us to surrender camera film and placed us briefly under armed guard. We were requested to leave.

Back in Panama City, our inquiries received varied responses. A Pentagon spokesman assured us Special Forces never eat MREs on operations. The head of Special Operations in Panama contradicted that view but denied US troops were patrolling the border. Other experts confirmed our suspicions. The US and Panama were signing new drug co-operation agreements that would grant the Americans far wider powers in Panama. Indeed the US appears to be turning Panama into a major platform for President Bush's new policy priority, the war on drugs.

Panamanian officials expressed no knowledge of the Special Forces operation. But neither did they express anger or surprise. One interrupted a question saying, "You seem to forget. We've been invaded."

Colombia came through its presidential elections in May with fragile hopes for peace won at a high cost in lives. From the mountain capital, Bogota, Robin Dilks reviewed the formidable agenda of the President-elect, Mr Cesar Gaviria.

DEATH, DRUGS AND DEMOCRACY

ROBIN DILKS   BOGOTA   28 MAY 1990

P ale sunshine illuminates the wooded cliffs above the city; everything in the streets is brightly painted; a bus in red and yellow livery blows soot across the pavement as it heaves into second gear. Later, bombs or no bombs, the raunchy music will blare out from the bars, but many will be almost empty. The day after the elections is a holiday; after heroic work to publish the results in record time, the count stopped at 93% - even election officials are taking the day off.

The urbane President-elect, Mr Cesar Gaviria, went to play tennis. The mood, though, is distinctly downbeat, a measure of scepticism that the elections can really change anything. At 43 Mr Gaviria is a political prodigy who's had the presidency thrust upon him. He dedicated his victory to the three other aspirants slain during the campaign, especially to Senator Luis Carlos Galan, the great hope of the renewal faction of the Liberal Party. Galan was assassinated at a campaign rally in August 1989, almost certainly on the orders of the drugs traffickers. Gaviria had been his campaign manager, he had no intention to run for the presidency. But at the funeral Galan's son proclaimed him his political heir to promote reform and modernisation, to stand against corruption and concessions to the traffickers.

Gaviria also inherited the death threats. He's an economist with a quick brain, a sardonic sense of humour, a young family and a past passion for the

196

Beatles. His first names are Cesar Augusto after the Roman Emperor Caesar Augustus. Gaviria has a clear idea of what needs to be done to lead Colombia out of its interminable bloodletting, lawlessness and poverty. He joins the new generation of Latin American leaders more in tune with the times, less grandiose but more pragmatic. But he lacks the legions of his imperial namesake. Private armies and millions of dollars to recruit hit-men are not the only protection enjoyed by the cocaine mafia. The town of Medellin is terrorised and building the political will to resist that is extraordinarily difficult. That's the view of a United States Embassy official; according to another, the biggest drug baron Pablo Escobar has infiltrated people, he owns politicians. He's able to move around the north zone of the city, usually one step ahead of his pursuers.

I n the elections around half the votes went to Mr Gaviria's rivals. All three favoured exploring some sort of accommodation with the traffickers. The country is divided on the issue. Critics of the government's offensive say it's senseless and unwinnable. Mr Gaviria rules out concessions. He says the government will crush narco-terrorism, but the commercial side of the cocaine business depends on more international co-operation; much more needs to be done to curb the consumer end of the business - after all that's where the profits come from. He plans to rebuild a terrorised judiciary, to make it rapid and effective, and to streamline the uncoordinated agencies of intelligence-gathering. He foresees a suspension of some constitutional guarantees to enhance the powers of the state.

There are also the left-wing insurgents who attacked polling stations, burned ballots and killed police during the elections; and the paramilitary self-defence groups, sometimes in league with the army, used for repression in the countryside. The promise of overdue political reform does offer hope for demobilising at least some of the guerillas which could give Colombia's dispossessed more say.

Mr Gaviria has an enormously daunting task and a lot depends on him. When he went to play tennis the court was surrounded by more than a hundred bodyguards. He'll probably be spending much of the interim period abroad, out of the firing line. So, after Colombia's elections, there are rays of hope - and a lot of trepidation.

During Global Environment Week in June, a lot of attention was focused on the destruction of the rainforests in Brazil. But in Rio de Janeiro, the Brazilians are worried that it is the urban jungle which is threatening to destroy what was once called 'the Garden of Eden'.

THE PERILS OF LIVING IN RIO

SIMON FISHER   RIO DE JANEIRO   JUNE 6 1990

U ntil someone pointed out recently that this was not a good way to promote tourism, visitors to Rio de Janeiro were greeted at the airport by announcements warning of pickpockets and thieves.

Well, forewarned may be forearmed, but ignorance can also be bliss, or so the authorities appear to believe. Rio de Janeiro is indeed suffering a serious image problem these days, and tourism is being hurt accordingly. The thing is that tourism is one of the city's most important industries.

While on the beach at Copacabana, it is not recommended to carry any more money than it takes to buy an ice-cream, and bathers walk the nearby streets in nothing but swimsuits so as not to leave even a pair of flip-flops on the sand when they pop in to splash in the surf - the chances are that they wouldn't be there when they got back.

The girl from Ipanema is still tall-and-tan-and-young-and-lovely, but there's a chance that if you get to know her well she may turn out not to be a girl at all, and her attentions are more likely to be fanned by the desire to take your wallet, than by your irresistible charm and devastating physique.

This is a country with one of the world's sharpest divides between rich and poor, and it is perhaps not surprising that tourists are fair game to petty criminals. Many are no more than children, and most tourists can probably afford to contribute a few dollars to bridging the gap. What is more worrying, however, is the level of violence. Stories of tourists robbed at knife-point five times in four days, or of pistol-wielding thieves forcing their way into hotel rooms, are not uncommon.

For the Cariocas, as the inhabitants of Rio de Janeiro are known, the problem is even worse. Fear has become an industry in Rio and security firms are riding a boom. A wave of kidnappings has shaken the middle classes, as businessmen are abducted by gangs demanding million-dollar ransoms. The victims are held in Rio's sprawling shanty-towns, fortresses where the police can only enter in force.

Ironically, some of the blame for the deteriorating situation may lie with the government's economic austerity plan, launched shortly after it took office last March. The plan froze bank accounts throughout Brazil, and even Rio's gangs of drug dealers were pitched into a liquidity crisis. The response has been a surge in crime and kidnappings which the police have been unable to check. Part of the reason for that is the fact that some policemen have been working with the gangs. Brazilian policemen earn about 150 dollars per month, which means that many supplement their derisory income by breaking the law. At least eight members of the police anti-kidnapping squad are currently under arrest for extortion.

For those too poor to be held for million-dollar ransoms, there are other daily problems to face. Like deciding which of a dozen different inflation indices to trust after the new government abolished the official index and declared that inflation was now zero. Prices are still going up in the shops but wages are static and the last official monthly inflation figure, a staggering 84% for March, seems to have been wiped from the accounts - at least as far as those who expected to get their matching monthly wage-rise in April are concerned. Consequently, the government is now facing a wave of strikes.

But lest I give the impression that life in Rio de Janeiro is an obstacle course with disaster looming at every turn, it is worth mentioning that Carnival this year was repeated - at least as long as the Brazilian team were playing in the World Cup.

Fernando Collor de Mello assumed office in April as Brazil's president for a five-year term in which he's promised to transform the country. His economic reform programme has already had an enormous domestic impact. But many Brazilians were still not sure what to make of their 40-year old leader.

BRAZIL'S PLAYBOY PRESIDENT

ROBIN DILKS   SAO PAULO   18 JUNE 1990

O n Sunday he donned the jumpsuit and helmet of an aeronaut to break the sound barrier in an airforce jet. By Tuesday he was pushing a supermarket shopping trolley in Brasilia and buying a basket of basic foods to convince doubters that inflation had stopped. One gossip columnist immediately likened Mr Collor de Mello to Superman and his down-to-earth alter ego, Clark Kent. These are not the only publicity and sporting stunts practised by the new president, who's making his predecessor, Mr Jose Sarney, look like a dreamer in a tropical hammock.

On a visit to Tokyo, Fernando Collor, a karate blackbelt, trained with Japanese practitioners of the martial art. In the Moscow frost, he made a point of going jogging. There's been more very strenuous jogging since, leaving the Brasilia camera crews wishing they had desk jobs. The president also rode a 1000 cc imported red motorbike at high speed around Brasilia. One weekend a parachutist staged a jump to land in the president's back garden - but Mr Collor was dissuaded from trying to repeat the feat himself. He did, however, have a perilous outing on a motorised hang glider.

The cameras of Brazil's biggest network, TV Globo, are always there. The evening television news is full of these images of effort, determination, energy, of accomplishing heroic feats. The president's speeches also reflect a will to overcome tough challenges. On taking office: "The number one goal of my first year as president is not to contain inflation - but to liquidate it." From the same speech: "My generation refuses to accept a Brazil which is an economic giant but a social pygmy."

His workstyle is economical. The president likes to get straight to the point, to hear opinions, check data on his computer screen, and decide there and then. Getting revolutionary decisions carried out by the glutinous bureaucracy is another matter - but again TV Globo helps create the right climate. The baddies are being exposed. First it was price gougers, then tax evaders; currently, it's the tens of thousands of local politicians who have been slow in adapting to the new moral climate; they still vote themselves handsome perks on top of outrageous salaries.

So far President Collor has succeeded in keeping himself in the public eye, in creating facts. Some accuse him of creating a leadership cult. One critic reckons the journey beyond the speed of sound cost at least a hundred and fifty thousand dollars. Another respected columnist reports a consensus that these presidential stunts are both a threat to political stability, in that Mr Collor de Mello is putting his life at risk, and maybe a symptom of psychological disturbance. But - says this writer - there's no doubting that people like it. That too is causing stress, according to the Institute of Psychology at the University of Sao Paulo. It's not only that anyone with bank accounts has had rather a lot of money locked out of reach by the Central Bank for eighteen months. The psychologists detect disorientation, because people are being persuaded that these are good times, with inflation beaten once and for all, while many costs have in fact risen steeply.

But the crusading president may meet his match in the person of his 74-year old mother. Mrs Leda Collor can be just as forthright as her son. She has palpitations every time she sees him indulging his boyhood hero fantasies. "Enough of these dangerous larks," she said in Sao Paulo - and urged the public to send complaining letters to the Palace. Mr Collor de Mello has agreed to give up the motorbike rides. But his image makers have plenty of other ideas. The president trained with the World Cup Soccer squad near Rio. Then he'll be diving in a nuclear submarine. If the economic transformation works, the rest of the world will have to sit up and take notice.

Recent political changes in Central America have brought pro-American governments to power throughout the region; but in June, American interests took a heavy blow in a three-month old banana war in a small corner of Honduras. According to David Adams, the banana-skin theory of history is alive and well in Honduras.

BANANA WAR IN HONDURAS

DAVID ADAMS   TEGUCIGALPA   23 JUNE 1990

O n July 20th 1920 Luis Melara, legal adviser to the government of Honduras, received a letter from a Mr H.V. Rolston of the Board of Directors of United Fruit, the American-based trans-national company.

The letter arrived with a luxurious gift for the wife of Honduras's president. It then went on to lay down a 10-point outline of United Fruit's objectives in investing in Honduras. They amounted to little less than a take-over of some of the richest land in the country and an ironclad monopoly over banana exports, worth millions of dollars.

That letter set the tone of relations between United Fruit and the Honduran government for the next seven decades. Its publication years later caused a scandal. During that time there were other outrages. The most dramatic came in 1975 when United Fruit president, Eli Black, authorised a one and a quarter million dollar bribe to Honduras officials. Shortly before the matter hit the newspapers, Mr Black fell out of his New York office window, in a suspected suicide. Soon after, the Honduran government paid a price too, victim of a coup attempt.

But the days when United Fruit made and unmade Honduran governments, turning the country into the original banana republic, appear to have finally ended. United Fruit is now called Chiquita Brands. Now they

202

won't be the only people selling Honduran bananas. Earlier in June a historic agreement was reached between Chiquita and the Anglo-Irish company, Fyffes, to share the produce of Honduran banana growers.

The deal came after the two companies had waged virtual war over the right to buy the bananas in Honduras. Fyffes complained that their bananas were being stolen at gunpoint and that Honduran officials were being paid bribes by Chiquita not to permit Fyffes ships to load fruit.

Fyffes officials were forced into hiding, taking out hotel rooms under false names and hiring armed bodyguards. Some even carried 90,000-volt stun guns for their protection. Chiquita accused Fyffes of bribing producers to break contracts with the American firm. They said Fyffes were guilty of commercial piracy.

Honduran dock workers are no strangers to piracy. Puerto Cortes, the Honduran north coast port where bananas are loaded onto refrigerated ships, was once the hunting ground of British buccaneers who seized gold on the Spanish main, 400 years ago.

Today, local people welcome the modern day buccaneers from Fyffes as liberators from the tyranny of the Americans. As I walked around the docks watching bananas being loaded for export to Europe, local workers described the recent events as the most historic day in their lives. It was a day many thought would never come.

The banana, or green gold as it is known, provides employment all the year round for local inhabitants. But it never paid well until today. Workers claim they were exploited by the Americans and forced to sell their produce far below what it was worth. Producers now working with Fyffes are earning up to 300% more than they ever did with the Americans.

If ever there was a banana-skin slip up, then this must be it. Fyffes may be a fast growing fruit exporter, yet, with total sales of $600 million a year it is dwarfed by Chiquita, who in 1989 alone sold $1.4 billion worth of bananas. But, and here's the rub, Fyffes was until 1986 a subsidiary of the Americans. And in September last year, Chiquita sold off a 20% interest it held in the company.

It's likely to be an expensive mistake as it sets a precedent which other enterprising companies may follow. And all at a time when demand for the banana has never been higher. Following the fall of the Berlin Wall and changes in other east European countries, new markets have been opened. Eastern Europe has never truly been introduced to the banana and fruit exporters are racing to fill the gap.

The Honduran banana war is unlikely to be the last.

For more than ten years leftist rebels in the tiny Central American country of El Salvador have waged a guerilla war against a much larger army trained and equipped by the United States. The justification for U.S. involvement has always been that the rebels are supplied by communist-bloc countries. But the rebels also have another source of money closer to home: coffee.

EL SALVADOR: THE POLITICS OF COFFEE

TOM GIBB   CERRO AL TIGRE   7 AUGUST 1990

A bout three years ago, I visited a big coffee plantation in eastern El Salvador where there had been reports of a big rebel attack. The plantation is about two hours drive from the capital on the slopes of Cerro el Tigre, or Tiger Mountain. It's one of the many volcanoes that tower out of the coastal plain. We drove up dirt roads through the thick coffee bushes, a canopy of protective trees above.

The plantation was a mess - coffee picking had stopped. Several of the charred outhouses were still smoking. Painted rebel slogans urged the peasants to join in the war against the rich. Spattered blood stains and bullet holes covering the walls were grim testimony to the battles that had been fought the previous night. The rebels had come down off the volcano and driven out the soldiers and large force of private guards, killing and wounding a number of them. They had destroyed most of the coffee crop. Four civilians, who had failed to heed rebel warnings to leave the farm that night, were killed in the fighting.

Shortly before I left one of the farm foremen drew me aside nervously - you know why the rebels attacked, he said in a whisper. It's because the senor didn't pay his war tax.

At the time the explanation didn't make a lot of sense - until I began to realise just how much both sides in the war rely on the coffee harvest. Coffee is the country's main export crop providing the government with millions of dollars annually. It has also made a small elite of landowning families fabulously wealthy. But few of these landlords can live on their farms. Instead they live in high walled mansions in the exclusive suburbs of San Salvador.

Since the war started the rebels have turned the upper slopes of the volcanoes into strongholds. The thick coffee groves provide cover from the air. Hidden minefields provide cover from ground troops. The rebels allow the farms to continue functioning - but at a price. Every year there are complicated negotiations, carried out with the peasants as go-betweens, to set the level of war tax the landlords will pay their guerilla enemies. On one farm alone the foreman told me the owner paid $60,000 US dollars. Nationwide that would multiply into hundreds of thousands, possibly millions.

Almost everyone pays the war tax and almost no-one admits it. It's the landlord's dirty secret. Workers on the plantation of the country's president, Alfredo Cristiani, say even he pays up rather than lose his crop.

The rebels also seek to gain support among the local peasants by forcing the landlords to pay higher wages. For many peasants the few dollars they can earn in the harvest is their only annual income.

Mind you, the rebels aren't the only ones to try to get a share of the loot. The response of some army colonels has often been to divert troops to protect the harvest - but they also require a price. It's one of the many ways the Salvadoran colonels have of making a bit of money on the side. "Extortion has become a national pastime," one coffee owner complained bitterly.

The war taxes give the rebels a large degree of self-sufficiency. In addition they get money from support groups in the United States and Europe and many of their explosives are home-made. But above all the taxes demonstrate the weakness of the government's writ in the large areas of the countryside. There is little the army can do about it.

This was emphasised a short time ago when I visited the rebel camps high up the slopes of Cerro el Tigre and asked them about the attack three years ago. They said the owner, supported by the army who wanted to break the system, had decided to use his money to set up his own security force rather than pay his war tax. Fearing a precedent the rebels attacked the farm.

"The owner's been very friendly ever since", the rebels said. "Now it's no problem".

Chile has been using its recently restored democratic freedoms to honour its former Marxist leader, Salvador Allende. President Allende was killed 17 years ago in the military coup which brought General Pinochet to power. Early in September his family was able at last to bury him with the full honours befitting a former head of state.

REMEMBERING ALLENDE

ROBIN DILKS   SANTIAGO   8 SEPTEMBER 1990

P eople who work with the families of the 'disappeared' in Latin America have said that not knowing what happened to a detained husband, son or daughter can sometimes be even worse than certain news of their deaths, however tragic that may be. Some relatives nourish hopes of finding their loved ones for decades, they can't grieve. They live on in permanent anxiety and can't really get on with their lives. Facing the truth about what happened is part of the therapy; and that's what's been happening in Chile since the formal end of the military dictatorship.

Gruesome deeds which were always denied are incontrovertibly coming to light. Re-burying Allende was part of that process. It brought some consolation to his widow and her two surviving daughters. Thousands lined the streets and filed past the pale and soaring stone slabs of the new mausoleum, many of them leaving red carnations in the crypt. The new tomb is in the capital's general cemetery a few yards from those of a dozen other former presidents of Chile.

The day after the coup in September 1973, Allende's body had been hastily buried in the resort city of Vine del Mar on the coast. The army did allow his widow, Hortensia Bussi, to attend that burial, but not his daughters.

The headstone bore another name. Three days later Mrs Allende went into exile in Mexico. She said that she had never expected the chance to give her husband a decent burial; this was an unexpected gift. In a dignified speech at the cemetery entrance, she said that mutual respect would not be restored while many other Chileans lay in lost graves. Chile owed them all the minimum recompense that was now being extended to Salvador Allende.

Admirers of Allende stress that he had been democratically elected; that he chose to die for his ideals rather than surrender, and that he believed strongly in social justice. Analytical articles in the left-wing press stress that he did have popular support; that in the hours before the coup he had decided to call a plebiscite to put his popularity to the test; and that he spoke of finding a distinctly Chilean route to socialism, certainly statist, but at the same time democratic and humanist. Supporters add bitterly that his marxist experiment for Chile stood little chance against the might of Nixon's White House and its dirty tricks.

But the dictatorship was long, it has only just ended, and General Pinochet is still army chief. So that generous judgement of Allende as a martyr of the enlightened left is very far from being a consensus view in Chile. Stung by the pro-Allende publicity, a leader of the newish pro-Pinochet party, the UDI, said the day after the funeral that Allende was the worst president Chile had had and he was to blame for the destruction of the economy and the breakdown of democracy. Others recalled the food shortages, the alienation of the middle class, the contrast between Allende's radical programme of government and his thinnest of mandates, and his failure to control the revolutionary zeal of parts of his heterogenous coalition.

This revival of traumatic memories on both sides held considerable risks for President Aylwin, whose political career illustrates the essence of Chilean politics: building a workable coalition from a mosaic of tendencies, which a makes a diagram of the evolution of political groups like a printed circuit. In 1973, Aylwin opposed Allende and he approved the congressional accusation of unconstitutional government which paved the way for the coup. Yet it was he, still a Christian Democrat, who led the centre-left coalition which defeated Pinochet in the key plebiscite on his government two years ago, leading to his election to succeed the two arch-adversaries.

The right tut-tutted over his presence at the funeral. Some socialists with long memories cannot forget or forgive his opposition to Allende. Part of his speech at the cemetery gates was greeted with derisive whistling - the Chilean equivalent of heckling. But as he has done before, Mr Aylwin silenced the sniping. As President of all Chileans he had to be there. "I was an opponent of Allende," he said, "and given the same circumstances I would be again. But the horrors and ruptures that we've lived through since have taught us that those circumstances must and cannot be repeated for whatever reason. And it's up to all of us to prevent that happening."

Mr Aylwin emerged from the event with enhanced standing. And he needs that to satisfy the expectations of a convalescent society from the very narrow political space marked out by General Pinochet.

SOUTH-EAST ASIA

December	1	1989	V.P. Singh elected Prime Minister of India
June	4	1990	1st Anniversary of Massacre at Tiananmen Square, Peking
August	6	1990	Dismissal on Corruption charges of President Benazir Bhutto of Pakistan, by President Ghulam Ishaq Khan
September	1	1990	Supreme Court of India rules it cannot implement controversial job reservation scheme for lower Castes
September	10	1990	Representatives of the Cambodian Government and 3 Guerilla groups agree to form a National Council in run-up to Cambodian Elections

Three months after the declaration of martial law in Peking, the Communist authorities had regained full control. There were signs, however, that student resistance had not been completely crushed, but forced underground.

PEKING AFTER TIANANMEN SQUARE

JAMES MILES   PEKING   30 AUGUST 1989

A t a park in north-eastern Peking, scores of Chinese gather every Sunday morning to practice their English. They stand among trees, in small groups, chattering to each other in text-book phrases. It is not a place for the timid. Go there as a foreigner and you will be pounced on by eager young students and bombarded with questions - what do you think of Mrs Thatcher? How do you like Peking?

A few days ago I went to visit the English-speaking corner for the first time since the army crackdown in June. As I approached the crowds, I expected that this time they would be too afraid to talk to a foreigner - after all, a Chinese worker had been sentenced to ten years in prison after speaking his mind about the massacre with American television - but as it turned out, I was very much mistaken.

I was surrounded by more than a dozen Chinese ranging from young college students to what appeared to be middle-aged intellectuals. Where was I on the night the army moved in, they wanted to know. What did I see? Did I think Hong Kong should become independent? Did I think the West should apply economic sanctions against China? I told them what I thought then, and it was my turn to question them. Did people believe in the government's propaganda about what happened in June? Old people maybe, replied one student, but not the young. Another said that those who didn't actually witness the events weren't frightened, because only a few people were affected by the current crack-down. I asked them whether another uprising could happen. A young student replied that China was still controlled by old men whose every sentence had to be obeyed. It is difficult to predict what would happen when they die, he said, but it is possible that something could happen then.

But the fact that they talked to me so openly was a sign that China's old techniques of repression are becoming less effective. To be sure, the repression continues - thousands of people have been arrested in Peking alone, and almost everyone in the city has been asked to write down or explain what their attitude was to the democracy movement, and what role they played in it.

But the hardline leadership is up against a people galvanised by a rare feeling of solidarity. At the height of the protest, nearly a million demonstrators were on the streets, and even some policemen were expressing their sympathy. Now people may be too scared to demonstrate in public, but privately many seem to be helping each other survive the crack-down, or simply laughing it off.

Government workers are being taken on outings to the military museum to see an exhibition that is officially called "The Suppression Of The Counter-Revolutionary Rebellion", but most of the visitors I saw paid little attention to the exhibits of military equipment, gazing instead, with barely concealed enthusiasm, at the pictures of demonstrators and anti-government posters. Some visitors even take notes from the dissident writings on display. And while official newspapers publish endless denunciations of Western trends, and call for the suppression of pornography and dissident literature, it seems almost business as usual at the book-stalls and Western-style bars.

At one university campus, it is even possible to buy books by authors now denounced as counter-revolutionaries, and whose works are said to poison the minds of the young. Biographies of the disgraced former leader of the Communist Party, Zhao Ziyang, are more difficult to find these days, but you can easily buy books about his predecessor, the late Hu Yaobang - who for a while was regarded by Democracy activists as a symbol of liberal values.

Since the army moved in, one or two of Peking's few Western-style bars have been closed down, but others are thriving, and there is even a new one called 'Starlights' just off Chiang Boulevard. There you can find youths with long hair and jeans disco-dancing to the deafening beat of live rock music, as soldiers with AK-47's patrol the street outside. As for the confessions that the authorities are requiring almost everyone in Peking to make, it is known that in at least some organisations it is enough simply to say that you oppose the demonstrations, even though your employers know otherwise. There are sinister stories too of employers being told by the authorities that their lists of suspects are not long enough, and to try and find some more.

After a long hot summer trying to remould the population, the authorities now face a new challenge with the start of the academic year. They have already adopted a series of measures to keep students in check, particularly at Peking University which has traditionally been regarded as the standard-bearer of student activism. There, first year students are now being required to do a year's military training before beginning their courses. The number of first-year places has been cut from two thousand to about eight hundred, and no new students are being admitted to courses in subjects such as political science and Chinese studies, which in the past have produced unusually large numbers of activists.

Of course, like everyone else in the country, students are being required to undergo expensive ideological education. But there are signs that the authorities are nervous. Without explanation, the start of term at Peking University has been delayed by more than a month until mid-October. One theory is that the loyalty of the teachers has to be established first, before the students can be allowed back.

The leadership could now be faced with a difficult choice; either to intensify the severity of the crack-down, or to make concessions to win back the support of the people. But for the time being although the street protests are over, it seems that their efforts to subdue Peking are proving less than effective.

In March China published figures showing that in 1989, customs officials seized five times more heroin than in 1988. The alarming rise in drug smuggling follows what appears to be a shift in the tactics used by drug producers in the infamous Golden Triangle area of Laos, Burma and Thailand. More and more, they are smuggling their product out through mainland China, through the south-western border province of Yunnan.

ON THE DRUG TRAIL IN CHINA

SIMON LONG   YUNNAN   9 MARCH 1990

Kunming, the capital city of Yunnan province, is a delightful place. The crisp sunshine and flower-laden streets have earned it the nickname 'The Spring-time City'. It is also surprisingly prosperous. The shops are well-stocked, and Kunming has seen a boom in the construction of modern offices and hotels. There is a gleaming new skyscraper in the centre of town housing a cultural centre. Inside you can catch musical performances, go disco-dancing, go to classes to learn English or traditional medical techniques, or join men and women in body-building classes.

But still, Kunming's streets are lined with hawkers. Yunnan boast 26 ethnic minorities, and many of the peasants and others selling their wares at the roadside are dressed in colourful and exotic national costumes. They sell everything from Thai-style hand-woven bags to pineapples and sunglasses, and they sell pipes. Some are big tubes of hollowed bamboo; some are small hand-decorated tin water-pipes. Asked what they are for, the vendors will say tobacco, but if you like, you can use them for opium. Yunnan is famous for its high quality tobacco.

Increasingly, however, this apparently idyllic town is drawing attention as one of the centres in China of resurgent illegal drug abuse. Before the victory of the communist revolution in 1949, one third of cultivated land in Yunnan was devoted to the opium poppy. Across China, in the early 1950s, drug addiction, once rampant, was virtually wiped out. But now it has reappeared, not just as opium smoking, but as heroin, with all its miserable trappings - the needles, the crime, the degradation, and even, in one part of Yunnan at least, the AIDS virus, transmitted by shared needles. So the friendly sunny streets of Kunming have a dark side.

Outside the town hall, a notice board warns of the dangers of drugs and AIDS, and manages to associate them with grotesque pictures of the effects of venereal diseases. In a back alley, a blackboard used for conveying the government's propaganda messages carries the neatly chalked confession of a heroin addict. It describes how when he started taking the drug his mouth was dry and his throat burned. In two weeks, he was hooked. He started cheating his wife out of the house-keeping money. His family finally turned him in to the police, after he tricked his mother into giving him by Chinese standards a huge sum of money for a fictitious medical operation for his son.

Last year the authorities in Kunming say they detained and tried to rehabilitate more than 2,000 addicts. The problem, they say, is that opium producers in the Golden Triangle area of Laos, Burma and Thailand are now sending more and more of the drug out onto the international market through their province. Yunnan's long, inaccessible borders are made up of rivers, mountains and jungle. For long stretches the very idea of Customs controls is far-fetched.

The Yunnan narcotics bureau has had some spectacular successes. A couple of years ago a large amount of heroin was seized when its owners were caught pushing it through a street in a country town in a wheelbarrow. But the money involved in the heroin trade raises another worry, that Yunnan's own people might start growing opium again, and even processing it into heroin.

It is, apparently, not difficult. Indeed, some reports say that is already happening. But the risks are high. Last year in Kunming, they arrested 430 people for drug trafficking. Figures were unavailable; but a significant proportion of those arrested will have been sentenced to death, and executed in the Chinese manner, with a single bullet in the back of the neck.

In Indochina the Communist government in Laos is accelerating its move towards an increasingly free market economy and is opening up still further to the outside world. The Communist rulers show no signs of agreeing to loosen their almost total grip on power.

LAOS - LAND OF A MILLION ELEPHANTS

ALEXANDER THOMSON   VIENTIANE   7 APRIL 1990

The markets in Vientiane are bustling once again; foreign investors are moving in at a faster rate than ever before. A home-grown version of hard rock can be heard at the Vienlati Nightclub, and fairy lights twinkle above the main hotel - the Lane Xang - the Hotel of a Million Elephants. But it still pays in business to have high level contacts in the Communist administration. The nightclub is a state-owned enterprise which must close before midnight. The fairy lights at the Lane Xang Hotel are in the shape of a hammer and sickle.

Laos may be opening up to the outside world; it may be adopting free market economic principles, but the old men whose stern faces stare down at you from office walls show no signs of weakening their grip on political power. They fought long and hard to get that power, as senior cadres in what was known as the *Pathet Lao*. They inherited a country - indeed a kingdom - which was one of the poorest in the world: a landlocked little backwater nestling between almost inaccessible mountains and the Mekong River. The country had been almost totally neglected by its former colonial masters, the French, who built few roads and even fewer schools. They were much more interested in their other Indo-Chinese possessions of Vietnam and Cambodia. Vientiane gained a reputation for lotus-eaters, opium smokers, adventurers and beautiful girls.

Whatever sleepy charm Vientiane may have had was rudely shattered when the backwater for a while edged close to the front-line in the Cold War. This was when the Americans moved in - in force but under cover - to run one of their more complex secret wars; to stop Laos becoming a domino. The CIA funded hill tribe armies, a murky combat airline, royalists, mercenaries, adventurers, and, it is alleged, drug barons. American planes bombed the Ho Chi Minh trail as it wove through Laos and repeatedly attacked one of the main battlegrounds - the Plain of Jars. Fortunes were funnelled in under US aid programmes; Vientiane became notorious in the region for its drugs, its bars with names like the Purple Porpoise, and its bizarre sexual practices performed, if one chose, over an evening meal.

W hen the puritanical Pathet Lao gained power, 15 years ago this year, all that changed. Hundreds of thousands of royalists and their followers, businessmen, professionals, indeed most of the elite, fled across the Mekong River. There is now little to show for the American or royal presence except for a few fading palaces, a few turkey farms and a thriving scrap metal business dealing in downed American aircraft and other wrecked equipment, particularly in the Plain of Jars. The small anti-personnel bombs the Americans dropped in their hundreds of thousands, when made safe, make unusual ashtrays, hub caps make good cooking pot covers, aluminium and steel can be easily worked by village blacksmiths. According to one Western aid worker I spoke to in Vientiane, when he asked a villager in the Plain of Jars what kind of help they needed, he was told that another scrap B52 would come in very useful.

American officials say the way crash sites have been disturbed for scrap metal has not helped their search for missing Americans, or MIAs, but Laotian government cooperation in the search for MIAs, its decision now to cooperate in the war against opium, and its release of many detainees from re-education camps are all key reasons for an improvement in relations between Washington and Vientiane. America's only embassy in Indo-China is expected gradually to expand. Laos is also improving its ties with China and opening up to its neighbour Thailand, the West and the Japanese as well.

So the markets are expected to bustle still further; more Thai businessmen are expected in town and their desire for Laotian girls may increasingly be overlooked. The French restaurant where one can enjoy salade aux lardons, steak tartare, and a very passable vin rouge to the sounds of Françoise Hardy should do better business and hotel bookings from tourists are up. But there are no signs for the moment at least of that twinkling hammer and sickle coming down from the Hotel of a Million Elephants.

*Despite some radical reforms in recent years, the government of Taiwan
still claims legitimacy over all of mainland China, as well as over the
twenty million people on Taiwan island itself. One of the most striking
demonstrations of this claim is the National Palace Museum, on the
outskirts of Taipei.*

TAIWAN'S
TREASURE HOUSE

SIMON LONG   TAIPEI   18 APRIL 1990

F ew would argue with its claim to be the greatest collection of Chinese
art anywhere. But is it also the world's largest collection of stolen
goods? On a leafy hill-side a few miles from Taipei, Taiwan's National Palace
Museum houses quite unimaginable treasures. More than 600,000 of them in
fact. There are intricate bronzes from early Chinese civilisations centuries
before Christ; nearly 27,000 pieces of porcelain; 5,000 jade carvings and
sculptures, 13,000 paintings, and so on.

Big as it is, the museum cannot display more than a tiny fraction of its
wares. The vast bulk of the art is stored in huge vaults, tunnelled into the hill-
side. The exhibitions are rotated every few months, but still, a curator told
me, it will be the next century before the museum has to start repeating itself.

Officially, the museum is just a provisional resting place. Taiwan's ruling
Nationalist Party, the Kuomintang, still clings to a constitution that says that,
one day, it will return to the mainland. The treasures are hostages captured in
a civil war that, technically, has never finished. Outside the museum stands a
black statue of the austere, bald figure of the former Nationalist leader
Generalissimo Chiang Kai-shek, gazing out over the hill-side, and perhaps
beyond, to mainland China. His dream of reconquering the mainland by

military force faded in the 1950s and 1960s. But he had its finest treasures.

The imperial collection dates back more than a thousand years, and swelled to its current bloated size during the last imperial dynasty, the Qing, who housed it in their palace in the Forbidden City in the centre of Peking. There it stayed until, in the 1930s it began a tortuous Odyssey across China, torn apart by Japanese invasion and civil war. In 1931, Japanese troops came dangerously close to Peking. The art collection was meticulously boxed up and labelled, and five train-loads with 20,000 priceless crates left Peking, for the new Kuomintang capital, in Nanking to the South. In 1937, the Japanese launched all-out invasion. Nanking fell with dreadful loss of life. But the art was back in its boxes again, criss-crossing China by train, lorry, ox-cart, raft and human shoulder. The Japanese surrender in 1945 brought the treasures back to Nanking.

But that period was just the prelude to Chiang Kai-shek's doomed civil war with Mao Zedong's communists. Again the 20,000 boxes were on the move, and as Chiang's new armies crumbled, a selection of the finest art was made, thinning it down to a mere 4,800 crates. They were shipped to Taiwan, the Kuomintang's last redoubt. For the government in Peking it was a straight-forward case of looting, on a scale never seen anywhere. Even the curator I spoke to said that the collection should be housed in the Forbidden City, which was left, in comparison, with artistic crumbs. But, she asked, what would have happened to the exhibits if they had been in Peking during the Cultural Revolution, when Red Guards went on an orgy of cultural vandalism? One day, the collection would be back there, she said. That, she added, was the hope of all Chinese. Many people in Taiwan do not share this wistful attachment to reunification with the mainland. So the museum is propaganda as well as culture.

The first exhibition is a photomontage comparing the history of Chinese and Western civilisations. It starts when Peking Man first stood up on two legs in 600,000 B.C., beating German Neanderthals to it by some 500,000 years. The exhibition seems designed to prove both that Chinese civilisation has always been ahead of the West, and that Taiwan is part of China, and now guardian of the Chinese cultural tradition.

In Indonesia, an unusual operation got underway in April to try to save the lives of a group of nine orang-utans which had become stranded in patches of forest surrounded by plantations. But an expedition organised by the Worldwide Fund for Nature attempted to capture the apes and take them to the Genung Leuser National Park.

SAVING THE ORANG-UTAN

CLAIRE BOLDERSON   JAKARTA   22 APRIL 1990

We started early in the blazing sun of a beautiful tropical day and drove through acres of small, evenly-spaced cocoa trees before reaching a patch of rough jungle. It was bordered on one side by a narrow river and on the other by barren scrubland recently cleared for plantation. In the middle, perched lazily in the top of one of the few remaining rainforest trees was an orang-utan. Reddish-brown, the size of a small human being, and with the expression of a wizened old man, he sat and surveyed us from his eyrie in the branches. Completely cut off from the rest of the forest, running out of food and standing in the way of the further development of the cocoa plantation, his days were numbered. And that's why some thirty-odd people were about to try to lure him down, net him and tranquillise him before driving him to the safety of the National Park.

But as the sun rose higher over the spectacular Sumatran mountains it became clear that it was going to be a long and arduous day. We ploughed through thick grass and bushes which disguised gullies and ravines several feet deep. We slithered over logs, frequently losing our footing, and waded up to our waists across the murky brown river.

The first task was to cut down all the trees and bushes surrounding the one the orang-utan was swinging in. That done, the animal's own tree was felled with a chain saw, the theory being that as the tree crashed to the ground, the orang-utan would run down it and into the waiting nets at the bottom. But it didn't. Orang-utans are said to have the intelligence of an average five-year old child. This one had thirty adult human beings outwitted time and again. He was built for jungle life, we weren't, and his thick strong arms and muscular legs easily outran his clumsy human pursuers. And that is the trouble with trying to catch wild orang-utans. The only people who have ever done it before are poachers and smugglers and their methods are crude and straightforward. They simply kill the adult apes and take the babies to sell in Jakarta's notorious bird market or to dealers overseas who recognise the value of the cute and cuddly, remarkably human-looking little creatures.

I t is that sort of action that has led the orang-utan to be put on the world's list of endangered species: there are just five thousand left, all of them living on the islands of Borneo and Sumatra. And it's not just the poachers that threaten the existence of one of man's closest relatives. The orang-utan's natural habitat is gradually being eroded by the widespread logging of the Indonesian and Malaysian rain forests. As the loggers move in, the apes have to move out. And if they can't make it to areas deeper inside the forest, they're usually shot or left to die through lack of food in the alien environment of scrub and cocoa trees.

This is just one more problem associated with the mass destruction that commercial logging reaps throughout the world, depriving the air of oxygen and emptying the land of wildlife. But, in Indonesia at least, there are signs that things are looking up. Thanks partly to the intense campaigning of international pressure groups, the plight of the orang-utan and many of his forest cohabiters has at last become an issue on Indonesia's list of priorities.

Conservation is no longer a dirty word used by do-gooders trying to interfere in the country's much heralded economic development. Wildlife is now officially recognised as part of the country's natural heritage and is protected by laws which ban the export of raw timber. Thanks to these laws, large areas of protected national park have been set aside which make the sale or export of protected species illegal.

It is not a policy motivated purely by altruism. There is a growing awareness in Indonesia that a rich animal life means a rich tourist industry, and a protected forest means a protected natural resource - and a good international image to boot. Of course, that doesn't stop the poachers and it doesn't stop the numerous cases of illegal logging which continue to carve up huge tracts of the Indonesian rainforest each year. There is criticism that reforestation laws are inadequate and rarely obeyed. But what it does mean is that, for the first time, the authorities are playing an active part in attempting to preserve the country's plant and animal life.

We were accompanied on our orang-utan rescue mission by Sumatra's head of forestry. His presence gave an official air to a project that might otherwise have been seen as just one more madcap attempt by environmentally-minded foreigners to save a bunch of cuddly animals. That didn't make the job any easier though. It was another twenty-four hours of hard work before the rescue team proved that it is possible to capture an orang-utan humanely and to give it a new chance for life.

The pace at which Communism has been swept aside in Eastern Europe has tended to shift the spotlight away from countries in the Far East where Marxist governments of one sort or another remain in power. As Jack Thompson reported, it is in Vietnam where, although the Communists cling to power, calls for a local version of Glasnost to accompany economic reform seem to be growing ever louder.

VIETNAM'S GLASNOST

JACK THOMPSON   SAIGON   4 MAY 1990

Openness has come to Vietnam but in a very indigenous form. The Vietnamese Communist Party remains in control but it has recognised the need for economic reform. The Vietnamese call it *doi moi*, or Renovation. The market has begun to rule. The peasant can trade more of his produce - that has led to an astonishing increase in agricultural output so that Vietnam is now one of the biggest exporters of rice in the world. Private shops and restaurants have opened not only in Saigon, the old capital of South Vietnam, where there has always been a tradition of rampant commercialism, but even in Hanoi, the very seat of Communist power.

As they have started to make money again, the Vietnamese have cast aside their fears of painful reprisal from the authorities. They talk, they criticise, they grumble, even in the state-controlled press. But they do it within limits defined by the party which has publicly set its face against the introduction of political pluralism. All of which makes it more intriguing to discover the phenomenon of "The Tradition of Resistance", a magazine produced unofficially by former members of South Vietnam's National Liberation Front who wholeheartedly allied themselves with the North

Vietnamese communists in the wars against the French and the Americans, only to discover that they would not be allowed to share power after the fall of Saigon in 1975. Rejected and disillusioned, they've maintained

judice silence - that is, until now. Their magazine has been surreptitiously circulating for about eighteen months.

As its editor, Nguyen Ho, wrote in an early edition, although it is not published in large numbers, "The Tradition of Resistance" reaches readers in many parts of Vietnam. In some places, copies are almost in tatters, having changed hands so often. In others, extracts are read out over the local radio station. So much for circulation - what about content? It must come as a shock to Hanoi's diehard Communists to know that ordinary Vietnamese are reading passages like this:

"Vietnam is today one of the poorest and most backward countries in the world. The image and prestige of the party, and of socialism, have been tarnished. This is a disaster. What is difficult to understand is that those who have committed mistakes have not been punished."

The writer went on to name five ministers who he said should be immediately sacked. Then he added with a flourish:

"The central element in renovation must be democratisation and openness. This is revolution, and revolution is the task of the masses."

The language retains Marxist overtones but for Vietnam it's bold stuff.

Then there was the article asking why the party never explained the removal eight years ago from the Politburo and from his post as Defence Minister of Vietnam's most celebrated general, Vo Nguyen Giap, the hero of Dien Bien Phu, the battle which saw the final defeat of French colonialism in Indo-China in 1954. Did they decide that after thirty years, he was the wrong man in the job? Had he made some unforgivable errors? And why did the man who replaced him last only a short time? Or was Giap, a popular figure in Vietnam, punished for being too critical of hardliners in the leadership like Le Duc Tho, Le Duan and Pham Van Dong? Even to ask these questions is like committing a communist version of blasphemy, or lese-majeste at the very least.

It probably means that openness in Vietnam is as unstoppable as *doi moi* has been. But this being Asia, it will not take a European form. For there is no country in what we from our London perspective call the Far East where a parliamentary system survives as an unadulterated copy of Westminster, not even in former British territories like Singapore and Malaysia. Vietnam is unlikely to become an Asian Poland, Hungary or Czechoslovakia.

Every now and then, the old guard in Hanoi kicks back and some outspoken critic is obliged to eat his words. But it looks as if they have left it too late. "The Tradition of Resistance" is now only one of several genies popping out of a Vietnamese bottle whose rigidly authoritarian cork long since rotted away.

*In Japan Emperor Akahito has delivered one of the country's strongest-
ever apologies for the role it played in colonizing much of Asia in the
1930s and 40s. The Emperor gave his apology to the South Korean
President Roh-Tae-Woo whilst he was on a state visit to Japan in May. This
new departure came only after several weeks of controversy.*

JAPAN'S EMPEROR REGRETS ...

GORDON BREWER   TOKYO   20 MAY 1990

Af005ter the official interview was over, one of Japan's right-wing
intellectuals was in a mood to confide. "Frankly," he sighed, "I'm
worried about our new emperor - I think he's a leftist." "A leftist?" "Yes. My
friends who know him personally say he's a pacifist and this intervention in
politics is very dangerous." "What intervention?" "Well, it's not just
apologising to the Koreans. For example on Green Day he planted a tree in
Nagasaki and said he wanted to save the environment. That's a hot political
issue. We do have our environmentalists here, but we also have people who
want to balance saving the environment with economic growth. And before
that he said he defended the Constitution - well many people here want to
change the Constitution the United States imposed on us, so that's
intervening in politics too."

My interviewee's parting shot was that Emperor Akahito should go back
to Kyoto - the home of the imperial family before the mid-nineteenth century
- and stay out of public life as much as possible. He didn't. Instead he
appeared the same evening at a state banquet with Roh-Tae-Woo - the
President of South Korea - and delivered what in Japanese terms was a
remarkably frank apology for the fact that Japan had occupied and generally

228

brutalised Korea for 35 years until 1945. "I think of the sufferings your people underwent during this unfortunate period which was brought about by my country and cannot but feel the deepest regret" he told President Roh.

It was the inclusion of the crucial words: "which was brought about by my country" which had Japan's right-wing so annoyed. Emperor Akahito's father Hirohito had apologised to the Koreans before, but he had simply regretted that there had been "an unfortunate past between the two countries.' As my right-wing friend was quick to point out, that statement at least left room for the possible suggestion that all there was to regret was that the Japanese got themselves mixed up with the Koreans in the first place.

The right-wing view isn't just fringe politics. For the past forty-five years, Japan has avoided the issue of who did what to whom in the 1930s and 1940s. It succeeded in giving the impression that the most unfortunate thing about the war was that Japan lost. The issue comes up regularly, and every time Japan's neighbours are just as angry. Each year a delegation of members of the Japanese cabinet pays its respects at the Yasukuni Shrine in Tokyo, where some of Japan's leading war criminals are buried. It's not an official delegation, but for the Koreans and Chinese that just compounds Japanese duplicity.

Added to that, the 70,000 Koreans who live in Japan, many of whom were brought to work in forced labour camps during the war years, suffer from a prejudice which often appears pointlessly insulting. The authorities in Hiroshima have only now allowed a memorial to the Koreans who died in the atomic bomb blasts to be placed inside the official peace park there. For years they had stuck by the ludicrous claim that there wasn't enough space and forced the statue to stay outside. Despite this change of heart, Koreans had a reminder of what they face in Japan when the memorial was defaced just before President Roh arrived in Tokyo. While that was the act of extremists, the simple fact is that racism and an ambiguous attitude towards history has been institutionalised at every level in Japanese society.

For several weeks before President Roh's visit it looked as if little had changed. The Secretary General of the ruling Liberal Democratic Party declared Emperor Akahito shouldn't go beyond his father's statement and the official spokesman at Japan's Foreign Office spent many hours attempting to explain to incredulous western journalists just why a forthright apology to the Koreans would breach the Japanese Constitution. But in the event the government, which wrote the Emperor's speech, delivered, and although the Koreans may not be entirely happy, there are signs Japan genuinely wants to make a break with the past. Prime Minister Toshiki Kaifu has been taking a whole series of bold initiatives in everything from relations with America to electoral reform, so the apology to the Koreans fits in with the pattern. After the Emperor's statement, the government was pointedly putting it about that a new generation of politicians was now in power which was prepared to face up to the past.

The new spirit seems to be catching on. On the evening of the Emperor's apology one of Japan's commercial television networks devoted its entire early evening news broadcast to Korea. It detailed the sufferings inflicted on the peninsula and talked of the 6,000 Koreans killed by the Japanese during a rebellion in 1919. But then it went further. "One of the problems is that many people in Japan don't know about this issue" said the presenter, holding up two books. One was a Korean school text book which contained 40 pages on the Japanese occupation. The other was a Japanese school text book. "It has only one page on the matter" the presenter said; "it doesn't even say how many people were killed." Later one of the young women in our office asked me for a copy of the videotape. She said no-one had ever taught her anything about Korea. Perhaps the next word should come from the Ministry of Education.

Barely a day goes by without reports of more violence in India's two troubled states of Jammu and Kashmir and Punjab. Is it something India will have to live with? Or is it possible to solve these crises with or without the consent of Pakistan - for it is Pakistan India tends to blame for most of her trouble.

THE TROUBLED STATE OF PUNJAB

JACK THOMPSON   PUNJAB   15 JUNE 1990

The fields are green with rice, sugar cane, maize and chillies. There are orange orchards and mango trees and water buffalo with soulful eyes. This is rural Punjab - the state bordering the province of the same name in Pakistan - the land of the five rivers. For like British India itself, Punjab was divided in two when partition came in 1947.

Today Indian Punjab is to a large extent the land of the Sikhs - although not all Punjabi speakers subscribe to the faith of the gurus, preferring instead the ancient gods of Hinduism. But the turban of the male Sikh is in evidence all over the state: in industrial cities like Jullundur and Ludhiana, their factories belching forth thick black smoke to enhance India's reputation as one of the world's big polluters, and in Amritsar, the site of the Sikhs' holiest shrine, the Golden Temple. It is there too in the villages and in the fertile fields that surround them. Punjab is a prosperous state. India would be hard put to feed herself without the enterprise and hard work of Punjabi farmers.

But troubled it is - by a kind of confusion born of the inability of Punjabis - Sikhs and Hindus alike, to elect a stable state government that all can accept. Taking advantage of this are the militants deriving their inspiration from Sant Jarnail Singh Bhindranwale - the Sikh Khomeini, as he's been

231

somewhat inaccurately dubbed - killed in Operation Bluestar, the Indian Army's fearsome attack on the Golden Temple in 1984.

The placid rice fields around the small town of Tarn Taran, for instance, are disturbed at night by attacks on police posts and civilians labelled as government sympathisers. But the response of the security forces breeds a counterbalancing resentment. The police are not averse to corruption - hauling off some youngster who'll only be released when his father pays a two-thousand rupee bribe, or hunting down small groups of extremists simply in order to shoot them dead but claiming the militants fired first.

It is in such an atmosphere that the Punjabis continue to harvest their crops, turn out steel girders, ball bearings and furniture in their small-scale factories, sell their wares in innumerable poky little shops, or earn a pittance as a rickshaw driver. It is in such an atmosphere that a smattering of Sikhs continue to worship at the Golden Temple even though they must run the gauntlet of a police picket line at its entrance, manned by men from other parts of India, suspicious of the ceremonies within.

I s Pakistan really to blame for all this? There is little doubt that the Sikh extremists in Punjab get many of their weapons from across the border. And Pakistan is the known base of post-Bhindranwale Sikh leaders like Doctor Sohan Singh, now in his seventies and a former director of medical services in the state; or Gurbachan Singh Manochal, who once served proudly in the Indian Army - from such impeccable credentials comes a hatred of Delhi provoked by the memory of Operation Bluestar.

Under these men is a bewildering array of armed groups with names like the Bhindranwale Tigers or the Khalistan Commando Force - Khalistan is the homeland the extremists yearn to create for themselves. These days they do not control the Golden Temple which is back in the hands of the grandly named Shiromani Gurudwara Prabandhak Committee, a sort of Sikh religious parliament, dominated by their Akali party. Even the Akalis are split three ways, with a militant faction linked to the fighters in the fields.

If the Sikhs themselves are befuddled by this, how much more difficult is it for outsiders to know what the community really wants? The Indian prime minister Mr V.P. Singh - no Sikh despite his name - has committed himself to elections in Punjab. All rational opinion seems to agree that this is better than prolonging central government control which formally expires in November. But will elections clear away the confusion? And will they bring peace? It may be trite to say it but it is nonetheless true that the solution must be in the hands of the Punjabi Sikhs and their Hindu neighbours. Mr V.P. Singh is hoping the Punjabis will see it that way too instead of clamouring for bold steps from the centre.

Mrs Indira Gandhi took a bold step in launching Operation Bluestar six years ago. Four and a half months later, she was dead - shot by the very Sikh guards she had come to trust.

Secessionist movements are a major problem for the minority government of Mr V.P. Singh in India. The tea-growing state of Assam in the north-east has recently joined Punjab and Kashmir in the north-west as a base for violent, separatist agitation, posing a serious threat to one of India's biggest exports: tea.

TEA AND SEPARATISM IN ASSAM

MARK TULLY   30 JUNE 1990

A separatist organisation has already murdered the chairman of one of the tea companies and has threatened planters who come from outside Assam. It has also demanded large sums of money from the tea companies.

The government of India has just ordered all petrol stations to close on Sundays to cut its bill for imported petroleum products. It is refusing to import edible oil to stabilise the price of that essential part of almost every Indian's grocery basket. It is attempting to juggle with tea auctions to keep the export price up and the domestic price down. But it is doing nothing about the serious threat to one of India's biggest foreign exchange earners - the Assam tea gardens.

Assam produces twenty per cent of the world's tea and fifty per cent of India's tea. World prices are excellent especially for Assam which is famed for what tea tasters call its liquor. The region was a backwater of British India and it has remained so after independence. In fact, one of the most common complaints you hear in Gauhati, its largest town, is that Assam is a colony of Delhi. This belief has spawned the Assam United Liberation Front, and the threat to the tea industry. It is a neo-Marxist organisation led by young men, some of whom have been trained by rebels across the border in Burma. Its cadres have set up what amount to parallel administrations in parts of Assam.

ULFA is popular in the villages because unlike the government, it does work. I was taken to villages where young men from ULFA were teaching children, helping farmers to grow a second crop, mending roads, and even reforming men who had taken to drink. It is popular among the young students in the towns because there is much to be said for its claim that the central government is exploiting Assam. Assam provides timber, tea and oil. But India has not reciprocated by investing in the state. The bridge across the Brahmaputra and the other investments which have been made have all been wrung out of a reluctant central government by agitation.

Assamese believe this is because India has never been fully confident that it can retain Assam. They remember Nehru's broadcast when the Chinese army invaded the north east. He said his heart went out to the people of Assam but they took that as saying goodbye. They point out that Assam is still the only major state which foreigners need special permits to visit. Assam's isolation is heightened by the difficulty of getting to the rest of India: the Tinsukia Express, one of the two trains from Delhi to Gauhati is known by railwaymen as the Dindukia or downtrodden express.

ULFA regards the tea companies as the epitome of exploitation. Sterling companies still remit handsome profits to London. The British tea planters have gone, but their successors come for the most part from north western India, the other side of the country. Labourers are no longer called coolies, but companies still treat the families who pluck tea, weed the gardens, and work in the factories, as their vassals. Conditions on the gardens have improved markedly, but cash wages are still low. Labourers do get houses, food, clothing, primary education, medical care, and even free cinema shows, and jobs are reserved for families living on the gardens. Nevertheless, the system is clearly designed to isolate tea garden labour which is non-Assamese from the politics, the questioning, the violence, and the disorder of life outside the gardens.

After ULFA murdered the chairman of one of the big sterling companies and threatened many of the planters, the industry turned to the Assam government for protection. But the Home Minister, realising that the tea industry is not popular and ULFA is, has refused to set the police on them. Rajiv Gandhi, who is also popular, accuses the central government of weakness in fighting secessionists in Kashmir and Punjab. He has told his party president in Assam to go soft on ULFA. Failing with the politicians, the tea companies negotiated with ULFA itself. The price of that protection was too high. They then turned to Delhi and to diplomatic representations in London. But the central government is unwilling to disturb its alliance with the government in Gauhati. In India politics comes before exports, and indeed everything else.

By July the latest outbreak of fighting between government forces and Tamil Tiger separatist rebels in the north and east of Sri Lanka had shown no sign of dying down. The army had made progress in the eastern province, but did not have sufficient manpower to control the entire area, and in the north, the Tigers were still on the offensive.

WHY THE TIGERS ARE STILL ON THE PROWL

CHRISTOPHER MORRIS   COLOMBO   10 JULY 1990

A few miles north of the town of Batticaloa, our car was stopped by a Japanese pick-up truck, painted in Tiger-striped camouflage. Five teenage boys armed with grenades and AK-47 rifles sat in the back, grinning furiously. Contrary to government reports from the east, the Tigers are still on the prowl. Many people have accused the rebels in Batticaloa of starting the war on their own initiative, by launching unprovoked attacks on police stations. But the area leader, Karikalan, told me that he had been in contact with the senior leadership in the northern town of Jaffna throughout the early stages of the conflict.

That came as no surprise. Preparations for war had been under way for some time - the Tigers had been building bunkers, laying minefields and stockpiling supplies. Behind the political façade of the year-long peace talks with the government, the Tigers were never willing to accept anything less than total independence. A generous helping of federalism, even de facto independence, would never have been enough.

The Liberation Tigers of Tamil Eelam, to give the Tigers their full name, were formed in 1972 by their current leader, Vellupillai Prabhakaran, to fight for Tamil rights. Four years later he took up the cause of a separate state for Tamil-speaking people in the north and east of the island, called Eelam or Homeland. Military confrontation with the Sri Lankan forces began in earnest in 1983 when the Tigers ambushed an army patrol in the Jaffna peninsula, killing thirteen Sinhalese soldiers. Anti-Tamil riots followed in the rest of the country, in which hundreds of people were killed, setting the tone of the conflict which has continued in various guises until the present day.

The Tigers are known for their discipline, ruthlessness and dedication to the cause. Even fourteen year-old boy soldiers wear the obligatory capsule of cyanide around their necks - suicide is preferable to the humiliation of surrender. The Tigers are also regarded by most observers as profoundly anti-pluralistic; anyone who opposes them, especially from rival Tamil groups, tends to end up dead. And throughout their negotiations with the government, a central demand was to be recognised as the sole legitimate representatives of the Tamil people.

But the Tigers have a problem. However much they might protest otherwise, they are essentially a military and not a political organisation. Even the leaders of the movement's political wing tend to wear Tiger-striped fatigues more suited to the traditional guerilla image. During times of war, support for the Tigers inevitably grows - they are seen then by many Tamils as their only protectors. And as bombs fall on civilian areas, the government's claim to be fighting the Tigers alone seems to wear rather thin. But as a political force, the Tigers are on less firm ground. And it could be argued that they need a state of perpetual war to retain their position of influence.

At the moment, they have just that. The Tigers' leader in Batticaloa, sitting in the remains of a war-ravaged village just outside the town, was optimistic. "This is becoming a people's struggle," he said. "They are getting ready for a long fight." Many Tamil civilians in the north-east might feel they have struggled long enough already. There is certainly a feeling of bitterness that war had begun again, when peace and reconstruction were so desperately needed. But many Tamils also seem to feel that they have no choice but to support the Tigers, in what they see as the latest cycle of a long-running ethnic battle.

Japan's booming economy has created a serious shortage of workers, spoiling school leavers and college graduates for choice when it comes to picking a career. This shortage has particularly affected recruitment to the country's armed forces - never a popular choice in postwar Japan.

NELSON AND THE KAMIKAZE

DAVID POWERS   TOKYO   21 JULY 1990

The first thing that strikes you as you walk up the white, marble staircase of the museum academy is a pair of carved bronze doors. The panels depict famous battle scenes from the turn of the century, when Japan's navy, founded barely thirty years earlier, stunned the rest of the world by defeating Russia. Rear-Admiral Yasuaki Imaizumi, who is in charge of the naval academy, has never seen the doors opened and has no idea what the room inside looks like, although he did play a part in bringing to Japan one of the highly revered objects in there. It is a lock of Nelson's hair.

Alongside it are two other locks of hair: one from Admiral Togo, the man who sank the Russian fleet, and who later became the personal tutor of the young Emperor Hirohito. The other belongs to Admiral Yamamoto, the mastermind of Japan's attack on Pearl Harbour. In the fanatical atmosphere of wartime Japan, the spirits of Admirals Togo and Yamamoto were worshipped as gods. Nelson, not being Japanese, was not accorded divine status; but Japan had originally modelled its navy closely on the British one, and even though Japan and Britain were at war, Nelson was still revered as one of the greatest seamen in history.

When Japan surrendered in 1945, the allied forces occupied the naval academy. Ten years later, when they handed it back, the lock of Nelson's hair was gone. Repeated requests were made to Britain for a replacement, and

239

eventually one was found. Rear-Admiral Imaizumi was given the job of carrying it back to Japan and restoring a curious part of Japanese naval tradition, but he has never even thought of opening the room and taking another look at Nelson's hair.

However, he becomes much more pensive when he walks into a room on the other side of the marble staircase. On the wall there, are inscribed the names of the 2,633 Japanese who died in suicide attacks as Kamikaze pilots or as human torpedoes. It may seem strange, says the Rear-Admiral, to have this memorial here, but the idea isn't to teach officer cadets to follow their example. The essence of strategy is not only to go out on a mission, he says, but to ensure there is a route back, it must be circular. The second half of that circle was missing for the Kamikaze.

A soft-spoken and thoughtful man, Rear-Admiral Imaizumi is concerned about a possible crisis of identity within Japan's modern armed forces - or Self Defence Forces, to give them their proper title. Japan's post-war constitution forbids the country to possess land, sea and air forces or other war potential. Subsequent court decisions have declared this doesn't exclude the right to self defence. But Japan's main opposition party, which made big gains in the last two general elections, still reserves its position on their legal status.

While such constitutional niceties exercise the minds of politicians and defence personnel, Japan's politically apathetic youth is more concerned with the good life - and the booming economy makes a life in the services decidedly unattractive. Wages and living conditions are poor - a sergeant with the American forces in Japan lives as well as a Japanese major. This year, one in six graduates of the Defence Academy decided to go into business rather than accept commissions with the armed forces; and altogether the forces are thirty thousand below their authorised strength of just over a quarter of a million.

One answer has been to encourage more women to join the forces, but there is considerable resistance to that in Japan's traditionally male-dominated society. Rear-Admiral Imaizumi thinks the answer is to give Japan's armed forces a visible target. Not war, but participation in United Nations peace-keeping forces. However, he says, that is not a decision the military can make. In today's Japan, it must be made by the politicians.

After long years of obscurity as a remote Soviet satellite, Mongolia had been hoping that the elections, coupled with a visit by the American Secretary of State, James Baker, would help provide a high-profile entree into the modern international arena. But it was not to be.

MONGOLIA GRAPPLES WITH DEMOCRACY

TIM LUARD   ULAN BATOR   8 AUGUST 1990

My plane from Moscow to Mongolia was packed with Bulgarians, Cubans, Poles and other members of what is still called the Socialist world, on their way to take part in a friendly boxing tournament. Somehow, they didn't seem as excited as I was about our exotic destination. One of them looked at the book I was reading - The Modern History of Mongolia - and dismissed it with a snort of derision: "Mongolia's modern history? It's just the same as all the rest of our countries. Mongolia has no modern history."

I began to see what he meant as soon as we arrived. The ancient Buddhist city of Urga had its name changed to Ulan Bator, or Red Hero, shortly after the Soviet-backed revolution of 1921. Now there is practically nothing in the Mongolian capital that doesn't look Russian, from the factories belching smoke in the Workers' District to the posters spouting the words of Lenin in a non-Mongolian, Russian-style script. Even the national hero, Genghis Khan, has been officially discredited.

But now the twin moods of the moment are democracy and nationalism. Like the East Europeans, the Mongolians have been given the go-ahead by

Moscow to take over the running of their own country. Everyone is ready for change, but they've been so closed off and so dependent for so long, they're not sure they can handle too much change too soon. No-one was too surprised, therefore, when the country's first multi-party elections returned the Communist Party to power.

Mongolians are hardly used to having a lot of choice. At mealtimes it's mutton or mutton. And at the election, the different parties all offered essentially the same policies - free-market reforms and improved human rights at home and a position of neutrality abroad. One party's manifesto was simply to make Mongolia rich and beautiful.

The main point of the election seemed to be to show that it could be held at all. The head of the electoral commission, Mongolia's only cosmonaut, had his work cut out explaining the complex voting system to the experienced international observers who attended - let alone to the nomadic herdsmen who make up more than half the country's two million population. Election officials who took ballot boxes round individual yurts, or tents, in rural areas, were treated as honoured guests and had to partake of green tea, dried yoghurt and fermented mare's milk at every stop, making the experience a tiring one for all concerned.

B ut if many Mongolians remained baffled by their first free elections, they may have found their first-ever visit by an American Secretary of State even more of a mystery. The visit was seen on the one hand as a prize for Mongolia's embrace of democracy, and on the other as a ticket to the wonders and riches of the Western world. Surrounded by the high-tech paraphernalia of another planet, James Baker swept in together with a small army of aides, secret servicemen and reporters, and plunged into a hectic schedule of hand-shaking, document initiating and dispensing of paternal advice on the market economy. But Mr Baker also brought with him news of the Iraqi invasion of Kuwait - and as the day progressed, it became increasingly obvious that the minds of the visiting party were not wholly focussed on such topics as the Mongolian Small People's Hural, or parliament. They were in fact deciding just how soon they could politely cut short the historic visit. Mongolia, having just been put on the map, was back off it.

But the locals weren't going to give up that easily. After the Mongolian Foreign Minister had duly agreed with Mr Baker's grave views on the Gulf crisis, the Secretary of State was led off to an open hillside on the green steppes outside Ulan Bator to witness a "nadam". This is a traditional round of festivities featuring the "three manly sports" of horse racing, wrestling and archery. This was how Genghis Khan used to celebrate his victories - and it soon became clear to anxious American officials that in terms of chaos, lack of security and the general slowness of proceedings, little had changed in the past 700 years. As Mongolian tribesmen whooped and hollered, Mr Baker ran out of polite questions to ask the gorgeously bedecked archers and disappeared into a nearby tent. His prolonged absence fuelled press speculation that he was being briefed on military manoeuvres of a different nature.

However, the manly sports of Mongolia were refusing to conform with the pressing demands of a modern international crisis. With Mr Baker back outside on the guest of honour's bench, smiling bravely as he looked at his watch, the final two wrestling contestants were proving an even match. Grunt as they might, locked in a timeless embrace, they were oblivious to their trainers' encouraging thwacks on their naked thighs. Finally, to the patent relief of Mr Baker and his party, one wrestler fell to the ground, and his victorious opponent began the graceful ritual of the eagle dance. His massive arms rose and fell, his movements mirrored by the hawks slowly circling in the blue sky above.

Suddenly, the Mongolians seemed to have salvaged something after all from the ruins of the visit. Finding their feet in the modern world may still take some time - but at least they are now free to rediscover their own history.

In August the 20-month old government of Benazir Bhutto was dismissed by the President of Pakistan. The only woman to head an Islamic government in modern times was accused of corruption and failing to maintain law and order. Those charges are frequently made against democratic government in a country which has for more than half of its history been ruled by generals.

THE FALL OF BENAZIR BHUTTO

MARK TULLY   PAKISTAN   14 AUGUST 1990

W hen General Zia ul Hak was trying Benazir Bhutto's father for murder after ousting him in a military coup, they used to say in the bazaars of Lahore: "There's one grave and two candidates for it."

That, being interpreted, meant: If Zia didn't get Bhutto, Bhutto would get him. Zia did get Bhutto and so there was a rather grisly historical parallel to the sight of the toothy, Terry Thomas-like grin of the general beaming down at me from vast hoardings when I arrived in Lahore on the day after the overthrow of Zulfikar Ali Bhutto's daughter, Benazir. The hoardings were to mark the second anniversary of Zia's death in an air crash. The man who proudly said to me: "you can call me a dictator because that's what I am" was everywhere to be seen. The young woman who had come to power through a democratic election was nowhere to be seen. The army had triumphed again.

Benazir Bhutto tried to draw a line between the army and military intelligence. She claims it was military intelligence which plotted her downfall and excuses the army because she still doesn't want to confront it. Those close to her say when she told the army commander about attempts by military intelligence to undermine the loyalty of her colleagues, he did nothing about it. The press, or some sections of it, had also been warning Benazir that it was the army which was plotting against her. But Ghulam Mustafa Jatoi - the politician who changed without a vote in the assembly or anywhere else from being leader of the opposition to prime minister, told a news conference that he was one hundred per cent certain the army had nothing to do with the president's decision to oust Benazir. The president, however, is a wily former bureaucrat who knows that real power doesn't lie in his hands, and it is very difficult to imagine that he would take such a step without at the very least consulting the army.

One of Pakistan's leading defence analysts has gone so far as to describe the ousting of Benazir as a joint military-presidential coup. The President's speech announcing the coup, if that is the right word, sounded distressingly familiar. The charges he repeated against Benazir were the charges made against all those earlier governments that had been ousted - and there have been plenty of them. The first charge was that hardy annual: corruption. Benazir told me she was very offended by that charge; she maintained that during her 20 months in power there had been no proof of corruption. The press was full of reports of rupees being made by everyone from Benazir's husband down, but as usual none of those reports were substantiated. Corruption there certainly was, but corruption there has always been. It will have to be seen whether the process of accountability the new prime minister has promised will prove his claim that under Benazir, Pakistan experienced the worst corruption in its history.

The other charge made by the President was failure to maintain law and order. Here we come to one possible reason for the army intervening. There has been violence and disorder in Benazir's home province of Sind and she called on the army to help curb it. The army wanted some of the powers it used to enjoy under martial law, but Benazir refused to go as far as that. The new prime minister immediately promised the army all the powers they needed in Sind.

Benazir Bhutto now faces the task of holding her party together and evolving a strategy to fight the elections promised in October. In this task she faces similar problems to her Indian neighbour, Rajiv Gandhi. They both head parties of sycophants and self-seekers which are only held together by the magic of their family names. The politicians who have come up the hard way and really know their craft are all in the opposition. Both leaders are themselves still inexperienced and so cannot compensate for their lack of political advice.

Benazir and Rajiv suffer from the same image problems too: they were educated in the west, they talk like westerners, look like westerners and have westernised friends. At least Benazir Bhutto doesn't have a western husband. Both have shown while in power that they can charm the outside world, but the same charm doesn't seem to work at home.

Benazir Bhutto now has to go back on the road to revive the magic of the Bhutto name. There have been almost no protests against her dismissal on the streets. And she only has until October 24th - if the President's promised general election comes off - to arouse Pakistan's anger. Many Pakistanis don't believe that Benazir Bhutto will be allowed to succeed at that. A defence analyst said to me: "The army has taken a corporate view that the Bhutto family is soft on India." A western diplomat took an even more sombre view: he said it looks as though no-one can rule Pakistan without the permission of the army.

A little-known rebellion in Indonesia's western-most province of Aceh has been occupying thousands of Indonesian troops trying to flush out a handful of armed men who have killed more than seventy people in four months. Most of the victims have been members of the armed forces or migrant workers from Java.

REBELLION IN ACEH

CLAIRE BOLDERSON   JAKARTA   20 AUGUST 1990

A ceh's rebellion is a story of violent grudges and elusive bandits that would be worthy of a place in a novel - if that is, anyone knew who the main characters were and what they really wanted. Aceh is certainly story-book rebel country. Endless ridges of volcanic mountains covered in thick rainforest stretch into the distance providing a perfect cover for the hit-and-run rebels who are currently persecuting the army and the non-Acehnese.

The image is now compounded by the large numbers of soldiers who have recently been flown in to stamp out the violence. Some five thousand extra military have been deployed in the last two or three months and they're making their presence felt. Convoys of armed and balaclaved troops charge ostentatiously down the middle of the roads escorting straggling bunches of suspected rebel sympathisers into custody. There are army check-points on the main routes into the industrial centre at Lhoksemawe, and helicopters are used to sweep the more inaccessible forest areas for suspected trouble makers.

This is not a strategy that's making the army very popular in Aceh, where the people are no strangers to confrontation. Staunchly Muslim and fiercely independent minded, the Acehnese put up a violent struggle against the colonial Dutch and were at the forefront of Indonesia's fight for independence. To put it bluntly, they don't like outsiders in Aceh and that sentiment seems in part to be behind the province's current problems.

In one of the most recent incident the rebels killed the head of an isolated village of transmigrants. The villager had originally come from Java, and under the terms of a government programme to ease the population burden there had been given help and hand-outs and been resettled in Aceh's sparsely populated interior. When their leaders was killed every one of them - some four hundred families - took the hint and simply packed up their bags and left. Now the village is totally deserted.

It's not that the Javanese villagers were obviously wealthier than their Acehnese neighbours. They weren't, as one look around the pathetically dejected shops and houses reveals. But, as far as the Acehnese are concerned the transmigrants have unfair advantages. "The Javanese come here and are given land, a house and food" one local told me. "They bring capital from Java and they work the same land that we work with nothing". It is a common complaint and one that has also been directed against those outsiders who, the Acehnese say, take the best jobs at the province's huge natural gas plant, its fertiliser factories and its other booming industries.

B ut while resentments certainly run deep, no one in Aceh really believes that the recent wave of killings is just a matter of economic grievances. Someone, they say, is pulling the strings. According to the Indonesian government, the attacks are all the work of common criminals and in part, it seems they could be right. More than forty soldiers were recently kicked out of the army for disciplinary offences. Some of them took to the hills to make a living growing and trading marijuana. But word came down from Jakarta that the Ganja trade had to stopped and the armed forces moved in to destroy the crops. The ex-soldiers having lost one living, then lost another. Harbouring a grudge, weapons and a good knowledge of local command posts they set about reaping revenge by attacking policemen and members of the army, capitalising on the intense anti-Javanese and anti-military feeling that already existed in the province to gain support.

It is also likely, locals say, that the former soldiers have joined up with remnants of an Islamic separatist group which briefly challenged Jakarta's rule and demanded independence during the 1970s. But the irony is that it is not really independence that the ordinary Acehnese want. They are proud of being Indonesian and proud of what they contributed to their country's fight against colonialism. It was gold donated by the Acehnese, they tell you repeatedly, that bought the Indonesian airforce its first plane, just as now it is gas mined in Aceh that buys Indonesia much of its badly needed dollars and yen. Aceh is a very rich province. However it is not the people, but the government and big businesses who have become rich. That is what is stirring Acehnese discontent and leads them to sympathise with an old cry for independence, and with a shadowy bunch of former soldiers out to get revenge.

In September the Supreme National Council in Cambodia brought together the Hun Sen government and three guerilla factions in its first meeting in Bankok. The Council is expected to take over Cambodia's UN seat from the Khmer Rouge-dominated guerilla coalition. But these bright hopes are not so clearly reflected by the mood of the country.

THE GHOST OF PEACE IN CAMBODIA

ALEXANDER THOMSON   PHNOM PENH   18 SEPTEMBER 1990

A new luxury hotel has opened in Phnom Penh on the banks of the Mekong river, and it looks so incongruous that the locals are talking about it landing from outer space. It's fully air-conditioned, has television in all rooms, lifts that work, a swimming pool and sauna, and a telephone system linked direct from the hotel to a satellite. This is all quite astonishing in this still-dilapidated city emptied by the Khmer Rouge fifteen years ago, a city still starved of western funds. This hotel is being regarded as a symbol of the city's regeneration, but if peace doesn't come soon, it could go bust - yet another optimistic dream that failed.

The drive from something almost surreal to the stark reality of Cambodia's suffering takes just over an hour. Kompong Speu Province is the closest the Khmer Rouge have come to the city, and the small, grubby, ill-equipped hospital has been kept busy with the casualties of war. During my visit, yet another of Cambodia's many mine victims was brought into the courtyard on a makeshift stretcher. One of his legs had been blown off while he was out collecting wood. His stump was covered in bloody rags, and as he lay there in the hot, muggy afternoon, clearly in pain but not uttering a sound, hospital staff stood around staring, chattering, smoking - there seemed little sense of rush. He was eventually taken in for an amputation, but the lack of urgency seemed extraordinary.

A young Australian nurse in Kompong Speu with the Red Cross said she too had been surprised at first by such apparent indifference; she spoke of patients having to wait until Cambodian doctors finished their siesta. One possible explanation is that Cambodians have learned to tolerate pain, and that war injuries have become somewhat routine. Years of suffering have blunted this country's feelings.

Up the road from Kompong Speu Hospital, and far along a bumpy dirt track, where only the other week a bullock cart had its wheels blown off by a mine, is another wretched product of the war: a camp for displaced people trying to find some safety away from fighting, artillery duels, mine-fields and the depredations of the Khmer Rouge. There are more than 100,000 displaced people in Cambodia - and that is just in addition to the quarter of a million, and more, refugees in Thailand - an increasingly unwilling host. They just want peace, but have become pawns in a war where control of people is as important as control of territory.

C onditions at the camp, called Okoki, are primitive to say the least and relief organisations are doing what they can to help. However, with the government promising benefits as a part of a hearts and minds campaign, some aid workers are wary of being too caught up in a politicised programme.

The suffering at Kompong Speu where control of people is as important as control of territory. Conditions at the camp, called Okoki, are primitive to say the least and relief organisations are doing what they can to help, but with the government promising benefits as part of a hearts and minds campaign, some aid workers are wary of being too caught up in a political programme.

The suffering at Kompong Speu, the abject misery at Okoki, can all seem far away from the bustling capital Phnom Penh, where shops and markets are busy and where every month there are more cars and motorcycles on the road.

But the basic economy remains weak and the apparent wealth largely comes from smuggling, black-marketeering and corruption - all major problems for a government at war; a government in which conservative hard-liners are asserting their authority over relatively reformist figures such as the young Prime Minister Hun Sen, whose main strength lies in his international diplomacy. He has stressed the importance of the Supreme National Council of Reconciliation, which has just helds its first meeting in Bangkok, and that meeting is something of a breakthrough.

But it is too early to speak of peace breaking out in this country, which has suffered so much for so many years. Hundreds of thousands have died. Many lie anonymously in mass graves. This past weekend those dead were remembered in Buddhist ceremonies by Cambodians who believe that their spirits are still hungry and abroad because no rituals could accompany their brutal death. It may be impossible to placate those hundreds of thousands of ghosts in a land which has been through almost every horror imaginable, but it is possible that with the peace process gaining momentum the horrors could be coming to an end. But hopes have been so often betrayed in the past that there's little overt optimism in Phnom Penh....that would, after all, be tempting fate where fate has not been kind.

Of all the countries outside the Middle East, Sri Lanka is one of the worst affected by the Gulf crisis. A quarter of its tea market has vanished, the price of oil imports has doubled and 100,000 of its citizens in Kuwait have lost their jobs. Meanwhile, the war against the Tamil Tigers continues.

THE SUFFERING OF SRI LANKA

JOHN RETTIE   COLUMBO   29 SEPTEMBER 1990

I first left Ceylon, as it was then called, when I was barely four years old, and I can't really say that when I went back there for the BBC in 1986, after an absence of 57 years, it felt anything like going home. It was rather like discovering a long-lost Shangri-la that you dimly remember in your dreams. But the dreams soon turned to nightmares, as I found myself daily reporting on the civil war, the massacres and the strife that had gripped the Sinhalese, Tamil and Muslim communities like a deadly plague. So it was with something like relief, tinged with great sadness, that I left the land of my birth two years later.

But this time it was different. The nightmares had faded, and happily I hadn't witnessed the carnage perpetrated on the Sinhalese in the south of the island last year, when tens of thousands of young men died in the security forces' gruesome battle against the Sinhalese guerilla group, the JVP. Bodies burning by the roadside, bodies floating down rivers - I'd read about them, of course, but you don't feel the same horror unless you've actually seen them.

In fact, I felt much more sadness from the death of just three close friends. One was Richard de Zoysa, a brilliant young Sinhalese journalist and television presenter, who was picked up by security men at dead of night last February, and whose body was found on the seashore next day with two bullet holes in his head. The others were Sam Panbimuttu and his wife Kala, two of the country's bravest and most visionary Tamils from the eastern town of Batticaloa. They were gunned down by the Tamil Tigers in the heart of Colombo last May. Despite all they had done for the Tamils, meticulously recording human rights violations for years on end, they were seen as traitors by the Tigers.

All the same, it was a happy homecoming. The many friends I'd made were so effusive that I felt more like a long-missed relative than a friend. Everything was so familiar. There was the majestic Galle Face Hotel, the British Empire's first great hostelry, still standing guard over Galle Face Green. In the breeze from the Indian Ocean that laps the Green's edge, young lads still send their delicate little kites dancing in the sky there, pausing only now and then to munch a chunk of pineapple or lick an ice-cream. Nothing seems to have changed.

High up in the central hill country where tea is king, I went once again to stay in the bungalow where I was born - a house built by my grandfather in a spot so skilfully chosen that you feel you're actually flying over the tea plantations that sweep down the valley to the river below. I went to my grandmother's grave in the church of a nearby town, and strangely felt for the first time that this really had been my home in infancy.

But all this happy familiarity couldn't hide the dreadful things that had happened last year. At a nearby tea estate which belonged to my family before nationalisation fifteen years ago, the factory that was busily producing beautiful tea when I last saw it, had been burned to the ground by the JVP. 24 estate managers had been shot, and many forced to flee their homes.

Now everything is quiet in the tea country, though reliable reports say that there is still some unrest in other parts of the south. I wonder how long that calm will reign. Already Tamils in the north and east are dying and suffering in a renewed war, said by human rights' sources to be even more cruel than during my time.

What will happen in the south when the full impact of the Gulf crisis hits Sri Lanka? About 100,000 families are no longer getting the money from Kuwait that supported them - that is half a million people. Their relatives will soon be back home looking for jobs that don't exist. The prospects for renewed social unrest among the Sinhalese in the south must be very real.

So how much longer can the Colombo elite flaunt their imported luxuries while the government pursues a civil war, all at the expense of foreign aid donors? How much longer can governments and many of their opponents resort to violence to solve political and social problems? And will India, whose chastened troops withdrew after failing to solve the conflict between Sinhalese and Tamils, forever stay indifferent to the instability off her southern shores? There is still no sign of a new approach to the island's development and internal conflicts. I left feeling sadder than ever.

This year, Japan set out its ideas on what will be left for the natural world in the remaining years of the twentieth century. A six-month exhibition, the International Garden and Greenery Exposition, was held in the industrial city of Osaka. Its aim was to achieve some kind of harmony between man and nature.

JAPAN CULTIVATES ITS GARDEN

ALEX KIRBY   OSAKA   28 SEPTEMBER 1990

The Exposition was certainly good box-office. It aimed to attract twenty million visitors, and looked like achieving it. The day I was there, with the sulphurous overcast day pressure-cooking the humidity into a rancid sauna, there were more than seventy-thousand people at the showground - and it felt like a lot more than that. I wondered how the demure young women at the open-air entrance booths managed to stay so pristine, until I saw that each was provided with an individual air-conditioner to blast her with instant chill, before it was swallowed up in the murk. I didn't grudge them their enviable gadgetry - I just hadn't really expected that a garden festival would rely so heavily on state-of-the-art technology.

But technology was very much the leit-motif of Expo 90 - which seemed in fact far less a garden festival than a showcase for Japanese industry and invention. Yes, there were flowers and patches of green. There were denominational gardens galore - the United Nations and the OECD were among those with their own plots. Of the national gardens, Britain's was the only one I saw that needed minatory signs telling you where to enter and where to leave. It had won a prize in the best garden category. It had not only a Henry Moore, but a work by another sculptor entitled - presumably by the artist - *Unacceptable Objects.*

Elsewhere, in the Japanese section, there were unsullied patches of gravel to rest the eye and to refresh the soul. There were waterfalls, caged birds, and miniaturised trees. There was an adventure playground for the children, with information in English handed out by captivating attendants entitled fairymates. And to whisk you round and through and over it all you could choose a steam train, a monorail, a train worked by magnetic levitation, or a cable car system. We did it on foot - and when we'd finished stumping damply through what gardens we could find, my jaundiced colleague was ready to write off Expo 90 as a rather poor theme park.

But then we came to the part of the showground given over specifically to industry, where many a Japanese household name was pavilioned in splendour, and surrounded by vast and infinitely patient queues. We had time for only one, the electric power pavilion, designed, according to its sponsors, to show how electricity will help to create a comfortable and fruitful society. Its centrepiece was a celebration of light.

W hatever I had expected, the reality went far beyond it. We were taken through the pavilion on a sort of conveyor belt with carriages - a comfortable and captive audience, kept firmly in our seats by the restraining bars which descend automatically to pin us in place. First the carriage climbed up ninety feet or so, through a transparent tube on the side of the building, before beginning its slow traverse down through every possible sort of spectacle - carpets and fields of tiny light-bulbs which changed in unison from one pastel shade to another as we passed, then a tunnel lit by pinpricks of violet, magenta and emerald. The we were running down through the midst of a titanic laser battle, with pulses of vermilion stabbing through the gloom, and replies shooting back in cobalt and gold. The finale was made up of a million points of light, a great sunburst of patterns and shapes and colours, an explosion of light, with correspondingly surreal music specially written by one of Japan's leading composers.

It was magical, it was deeply impressive - and it appeared to have not the slightest connection with Expo 90's stated theme, gardens and greenery. It was this abyss between theme and realisation that led some critics to damn the Expo, not simply as a tawdry theme park, but as a proud showcase for the products of Japanese industry that was brazenly sailing under false colours - conning the innocent and the environmentally pure in heart into visiting something which then trampled gleefully on all they hold most sacred. One enraged and possibly fairly typical critic - a Westerner, for what it's worth - castigated the Expo in print as a 'monstrous event', and one which showed just how warped was corporate Japan's perception of harmony between humanity and nature. He found it both aesthetically offensive, and a revelation of Japan's urge in the end not to revere nature, but to commercialize it.

I wonder, though. Much of Expo 90 was fairly unappealing, and where nature did get a look-in it was inevitably cribbed, cabined and confined. But I couldn't help feeling that that was probably, if unwittingly, an honest look at the future for Japan - and for most of the rest of us, too. Travelling around Osaka and Tokyo I was constantly struck, as a newcomer to Japan, by the very intensive use made of every piece of land - one report estimated the cost of a square metre in central Tokyo at a quarter of a million dollars. It is not uncommon to see three or four layers of traffic, on overlapping flyovers, themselves criss-crossing railways and rivers. And it is perfectly normal to see the tiniest open space on the smallest roof-top transformed by rocks, or bonsai, or even just plain grass, into a vestigial and defiant attempt at a garden.

There is not much room in Japan, and the frontiers are crowding in elsewhere. Perhaps nature, not only confined, but made digestible and subservient by technology, will soon turn out to be the only prospect for any of us. If you have seen Expo 90, then perhaps you can say you have seen the future - and that bonsai trees in raked gravel are all it has room for. I do wonder what Wordsworth would have made of it all.

AUSTRALASIA

The tide of mass tourism has swept into most corners of the world, and threatens to engulf the South Pacific. But on feudally-run Tonga the islanders seem refreshingly indifferent to the gaudy benefits it could bring.

LA DOLCE VITA
IN TONGA

MICHAEL PESCHARDT   TONGA   1 DECEMBER 1989

I n spirit, the Kingdom of Tonga is about as far from a bustling western economy as it is possible to get. The kingdom is a collection of tiny, palm-covered islands surrounded by coral reefs, set adrift in the South Pacific. There are long white beaches and sultry warm days, making rushing around quite impossible. There is what amounts to a national motto, an island philosophy of life. "In Tonga" my guide told me with a happy shrug, "if you want to sleep, you sleep." Under the trees the most common sight is, indeed, of people simply dozing their days away.

Two hundred years or so ago, the islands underwent the traumas of being discovered and settled by a variety of European adventurers. Now it is having to face another upheaval and dilemma: possible development as a tourist and industrial centre. Most of the other Pacific islands now boast the sort of ritzy tourist resorts found wherever the sun shines. Tonga is the last to fall in line... not because its government doesn't want the cash, but because in so many ways the country is a throwback to another age which modern business men and developers find hard to fathom.

To start with, the system of government takes some adjusting to. It is unashamedly feudal. The king has more or less absolute power. Without his say-so, nothing -but nothing - happens. His lands, which account for the vast majority of the island, are run for him by forty-two noble families. The ordinary Tongan people do not themselves own land. They pay an annual rent to their local noble. No money usually changes hands - they pay in kind with produce they have grown, or fish they have caught.

The king who heads this very structured world is now in his seventies. He is a large man in need of a stick to help him walk. I went to see him in his palace right on the beach in the capital, Nukalofa. His palace is a Victorian-style pavillion with a red domed roof. It has the air of an old English country house, and he likes to greet visitors while sitting on a splendid throne-like chair given to him as a gift by the British government.

All around are pictures and paintings of former kings and queens of Tonga in Western or tribal clothing, depending on their antiquity. A jovial man, he is immediately likeable and tells with relish a string of wickedly funny stories about the people he has met on visits to Britain and elsewhere. He has a liking for a great many of the material benefits the Western world can provide, and has his own huge satellite dish in the palace grounds. There is no television in Tonga, but he like to keep up with the latest American shows. He wants the country to develop and happily lists the help he has been given by foreign governments wanting to ensure good relations with this small, but strategically important nation in the Pacific.

"The British supplied the hospital" he says breezily; "the French the indoor athletic stadium. The Germans helped with the sea defences; the Australians are building the new airport runway and the Japanese the terminal. They're all doing a little," he says. But, smiling, he warns that despite the new airport he doesn't want to allow any flights in on a Sunday. On Sunday mornings, he told me, he likes to ride his bicycle along the runway and doesn't want to be disturbed by a string of noisy 747's trying not to land on top of him.

At a pinch, he probably would amend his training routine if tourism boomed. Whether this will come to pass is still a little in doubt: many of the Western businessmen I spoke to were becoming increasingly exasperated with life and attitudes there. It was impossible, they said, to convince local people of the benefits that industry could bring. New hotels and businesses would undoubtedly bring higher wages, but deep down the islanders are going to take a lot of convincing that the extra work will be worth all the trouble.

For Red Harrison, 1990 brought to an end his love affair with an aeroplane. Rising fuel costs and soaring aviation charges forced him to sell the twin-tailed, twin-engined silver Beechcraft he had bought in Nashville, Tennessee, and had flown back to his home in Sydney two years previously. The sale prompted memories of the most unusual journey of his life.

TIME GOES BY FOR THE BEECHCRAFT 18

RED HARRISON   SYDNEY   28TH SEPTEMBER 1990

There is a moment in long-distance flying when you know that death is only seconds away. That moment came for me high over the Bay of Bengal, five hours out of Madras, with the island of Sumatra another four hours over the horizon. We were cruising at 800 feet with the comforting, deep-throated rumble and smells that only old-fashioned radial engines can produce, when suddenly both propellors stopped.

There is nothing like total silence in an aircraft far out at sea, with no-one within hundreds of miles, to stimulate a flush of adrenalin. With a heavy fuel load, the aircraft had the gliding characteristics of a piano tumbling out of a second-story window. My heart thumped and at the same time, those wonderful engine noises came back with a roar.

What had happened? Quite simply, I had fallen asleep. Just for a second. It happens frequently among tired long-distance fliers. Close your eyes - and the silence is immediate. It is not unlike the phenomenon pilots describe as "automatic rough" - another hallucination which produces frightening engine noises as soon as the countryside below looks inhospitable.

There was plenty of unfriendly, inhospitable country between America and Australia. Even with modern navigation and communication aids, crossing the North Atlantic in a small aeroplane is not exactly routine, because if you miss your destination airport, there is generally nowhere else to go.

We fitted extra fuel tanks for the long flights over water, and the network of tubing inside the aircraft looked like a plumber's nightmare. Regretfully. I had to abandon the idea of smoking in the air. This Beechcraft was a flying Molotov cocktail.

But there was room to smile. Heading north from Tennessee, we spent a night at Sept Isles in northern Quebec, and the French-speaking authorities were decidedly unhappy when my Australian companion made the town rhyme with 'reptiles'.

Taking off at dawn became a habit, and I can certify that airport coffee at that hour is disgusting all over the world. At Goose Bay in Labrador, we landed as a snowstorm swept in, and the weather stayed foul for nearly a week. There is not much to do in Goose Bay, and my companion missed an education by staying away from the rough-and-tumble frontier bars. One bar had a juke-box which played the same record over and over. It was called: "The Squaws Along The Yukon Are Good Enough For Me." The words refused to leave me.

G oing north in Labrador, trees and vegetation soon disappear, and there is an eerie sensation that you are flying straight back into the Ice-Age - out over the ice-packs of the North Atlantic to Greenland - a place like no other country in the world. Greenland is a vast continent of ice nearly twelve thousand feet thick. It has a coastline of white mountains and valleys and rugged fjords, and it looks, frankly, terrifying to people in small planes.

Our destination was Narssarsuaq, a thin, black airstrip boxed in by glaciers sixty miles inland, up a narrow, twisting fjord. If you come from Australia, however, all fjords look alike. It would be easy to choose the wrong one and then, flying under low clouds, perhaps the story would end, because there is scarely room to turn and go back. But there is a trick about flying into Narssarsuaq that I learned from a novel by Ernest Gann. About thirty miles up the *right* fjord is the wreck of a Second World War cargo ship. If you don't see it, you are in the wrong place. We were lucky: ten minutes after leaving the coast, the nose of the freighter appeared black and sharp pointed in a light blue sea studded with icebergs, some as big and beautiful as cathedrals.

The whole flight took a month. From Greenland to Iceland, down to London, Rome, Heraklion, Luxor, Bahrain. Altogether, we made twenty-six landings before we shut down for the last time. And every port had a story. The Egyptian army posted a guard on the aircraft at Luxor - and charged us an American fortune. In oil-rich Bahrein, we couldn't buy oil for piston engines. In the Gulf, over the straits of Hormuz, we were shadowed for miles by jet fighters - nationality unknown. At Medan, in Sumatra, I fell and gashed a leg which, with the non-co-operation of some nasty tropical bugs, took more than a year to heal.

But most memorably this was a flight in which bureaucracies went berserk. Before you can fly yourself around the world, you must climb a mountain of paperwork. Getting permission to land or fly over various countries took nearly a year. On the flight itself, filling in forms in Karachi for customs, fuel, an overnight stay - took a mere eight hours in temperatures around forty-five degrees Celsius. The same procedures at Ahmedabad, in north-west India where it was even hotter, took longer. I even had to supply my mother's maiden name to buy fuel.

O bviously, many people must have asked the reason why. Why such a potentially hazardous flight? Why such an old aircraft (it was forty years old)? The answer lies in the film Casablanca, where everyone fell in love with Ingrid Bergman. I did, too, but I fell harder in the foggy closing scenes for the lines of the beautiful aircraft Ingrid Bergman climbed aboard after saying farewell to Humphrey Bogart. It was, I believe, a Beechcraft 18, and I've loved them ever since.

As for the flight, it had some glamour, of course. And someone had to do it. I will never forget taxiing into Sydney, the faces of the spectators hearing the window-shaking blast of those big, old-fashioned engines. It is a noise that comes from the heart of aviation. Sometimes just being a pilot is a wonderful feeling.

CONTRIBUTORS

Gordon Adam	Head of BBC Pashto Service
David Adams	Reports for the BBC from Panama City
Paul Adams	Reports for the BBC from Jerusalem
Donald Armour	Current Affairs Talks writer with the BBC World Service
Owen Bennett-Jones	Reports for the BBC from Bucharest and Sofia
Jonathan Birchall	Reporter with BBC World News, formerly BBC World Service Sports Correspondent
Elizabeth Blunt	BBC West Africa correspondent based in Abidjan
Alex Brodie	BBC Jerusalem Correspondent
Claire Bolderson	Reports for the BBC from Jakarta
Julian Borger	Reports for the BBC from Johannesburg
Malcolm Brabant	Reports for the BBC from Athens
Ben Bradshaw	BBC Berlin Correspondent
Mark Brayne	BBC World Service Diplomatic Correspondent, formerly based in Berlin, Vienna and Peking
Gordon Brewer	BBC Tokyo Correspondent
Harold Briley	BBC Defence Correspondent, World Service
Nicola Carslaw	Reports for the BBC from Eastern Europe
Adam Curtis	Duty Editor in BBC World Service News
Stephen Dalziel	Soviet Affairs Specialist, BBC World Service
Robin Dilks	BBC Latin America Correspondent
Mark Doyle	Reports for the BBC from West Africa
Sallie Ecroyd	Reports for the BBC from Budapest
Simon Fisher	Reports for the BBC from Rio de Janeiro
Tom Gibb	Reports for the BBC from El Salvador
Red Harrison	Reports for the BBC from Sydney
Roger Hearing	Reporter with BBC Radio News and Current Affairs
Peter Hiett	BBC North Africa Correspondent based in Tunis
Mary Hockaday	Reports for the BBC from Prague
Jane Howard	Reports for the BBC from Ankara
Stephen Jessel	BBC Paris Correspondent, formerly in Washington
Bridget Kendall	BBC Moscow Correspondent

Alex Kirby	BBC Environment Correspondent
Graham Leach	BBC Europe Correspondent
Tim Llewellyn	BBC Middle East Correspondent
Simon Long	Reports for the BBC from Peking
Tim Luard	Talks Writer with BBC Far Eastern Service, formerly BBC reporter from Peking
Martin Lumb	BBC reporter from the U.N., now with BBC World News
Barnaby Mason	BBC Cairo Correspondent
James Miles	BBC Peking Correspondent
James Morgan	BBC Economics Correspondent, World Service
Christopher Morris	Reports for the BBC from Sri Lanka
Tony Paterson	Formerly BBC Berlin Correspondent
Michael Peschardt	Formerly reporter for the BBC from Sydney
David Powers	Reports for the BBC from Tokyo
John Rettie	Formerly BBC Correspondent in Sri Lanka, now based in Moscow
Stephen Sackur	Reports for the BBC from the Middle East
Jasvinder Singh	Reporter for the BBC Eastern Service
Alexander Thomson	BBC South East Asia Correspondent
Jack Thompson	BBC Foreign Affairs Correspondent, World Service
Alan Tomlinson	BBC Caribbean Correspondent
Deepak Tripathi	Reports for the BBC from Afghanistan
Mark Tully	BBC Delhi Correspondent
Catherine Utley	Formerly BBC World Service UK Affairs Correspondent
Rick Wells	Reports for BBC Radio News and Current Affairs
Andrew Whitehead	BBC Political Correspondent, World Service
David Willey	BBC Rome Correspondent
Mike Wooldridge	BBC Southern Africa Correspondent
Nigel Wrench	Reported for the BBC from South Africa